SUCCESSFUL SEMINAR SELLING FOR FINANCIAL ADVISERS

SUCCESSFUL SEMINAR SELLING FOR FINANCIAL ADVISERS

The Financial Planner's Guide to Attracting Profitable New Leads through Seminars, Workshops & Client Events

By Philip Calvert

"It delivered massive value…"

"I bought Philip's book to get practical guidance on setting up our first seminar, and it delivered massive value. I never realised there was so much to consider, but this book goes into the science of setting up and marketing a successful seminar, in a practical and easy to use format. A must buy for any small business owner considering using seminars as part of their marketing strategy."

Martin Bamford, Chartered Financial Planner
Informed Choice Independent Financial Planners

"No-one comes close…"

"Nobody I have heard comes close to Phil's practical knowledge of using seminars and the internet (in all its varied forms) to get one's message out there."

David Crozier, Certified Financial Planner
Navigator Financial Planning

"…We worked with Philip Calvert on our seminar…"

"We ran our first seminar last night. The room capacity was for 50, and 61 turned up! 250 invitations were sent out - so we believe the return rate is pretty good. The mixture was roughly 60% new people and 40% existing clients"

Bill Hofstetter, Financial Planner
Inspirational Financial Management

ACKNOWLEDGEMENTS

For the tens of thousands of IFAs, Advisers and Financial Planners I've met over the last forty-two years.

Copyright © 2019 Philip Calvert. All Rights Reserved.

This book or any portion thereof may not be reproduced or used in any manner whatsoever without the express written permission of the publisher except for the use of brief quotations in a book review or scholarly journal.

Cover photo by Luis Quintero

ISBN: 978-1-70065-201-0

Contents

Introduction

- How this book came about

Part 1: Successful Seminar Selling: How to Plan, Prepare and Market Your Events

Problems Facing Small Businesses

- Funding for growth

The Need to Change and Adapt

- Thinking laterally

The Benefits of Seminar Selling

- What is Seminar Selling?
- Benefits of Seminar Selling to financial advisers
- Benefits of Seminar Selling to attendees
- The keys to success

Planning Your Seminars and Workshops

- When do I start planning my seminar?
- What are the five main decisions that need to be made?
- What are the five planning stages?
- Summary

The Golden Rules of Marketing Your Seminars

- Discover what works for you
- Don't rule out any particular method of promotion
- Make your event irresistible!
- Offer bonuses for attendance
- Get help!

Offline and Online Marketing and Promotion

- Offline promotion
- Television and radio advertising
- Telephone
- Direct mail
- Press advertising
- Audio and video
- SMS messaging
- Public relations (PR)
- General correspondence
- Online promotion
- Summary

How to Dramatically Increase Your Profits from Seminars

- Providing value
- Turning your talk into profit
- How will we cover the cost of each attendee?
- Consulting income (CI)
- Additional product income (API)
- Additional points about creating and selling products

How to Create Information-Based Products – Quickly

- Method 1
- Method 2

- Method 3
- Why will people buy these products?
- Exercise
- Summary

Part 2: Getting Your business Message Across with Impact, Power and Authority

Presentation is Everything

- Presenting an image
- Presentation skills

Confidence

- What are the factors that determine impact in a presentation?

Clarity

- Using different media
- A few words on using PowerPoint
- Storytelling

Conviction

- Characteristics of Presenters with Conviction

Connection

- Getting started
- Staying connected
- After the event

Part 3: What Happens Next?

Getting Feedback

- Formal feedback
- Informal feedback
- Summary

Following Up to Maximise Sales and Profits

- The next day
- Closer analysis
- Maximising sales and profits
- Summary

Some Final Thoughts

Confessions of a Mystery Shopper at a Financial Adviser's Seminar

- Summary
- The future

Taking Action

Disclaimer and Terms of Use

A Place for your Notes

Introduction

In this book, owners of financial advice businesses will discover a proactive, exciting, profitable and proven formula for attracting more of their ideal clients.

I am a huge believer in the common-sense notion that the amount of effort you put into your business determines the results you get out of it. It hopefully follows that if you positively and proactively set about increasing sales, you will be rewarded with great results.

But some ways of increasing sales are much more effective than others and this book reveals the secrets behind just one – one which offers potentially the greatest returns. And whilst the book is aimed at small financial advice businesses, the techniques and ideas included can equally apply to larger firms and networks.

The simple fact is, that many of the most successful financial advisers around the world incorporate seminars and client events as part of their proposition. It is a strategy that is consistently effective because it:

- Adds immense value to existing clients in a variety of ways
- Attracts high quality new clients
- Supercharges your referral enquiries
- Builds loyal advocates for your business amongst professional introducers and other interested parties
- Creates a valuable new income stream

'Seminar Selling' is not a new idea and many people will have participated in a seminar at some stage in their career.

Very few, however, continue with this marketing approach for a number of reasons – be it fear of public speaking, concern at the amount of organisation involved, the cost of holding the events or even lack of awareness of the potential benefits. This book will show you specifically:

- Why seminars and client events can be key to significant growth and profits

- The (considerable) benefits available to *all* small businesses – not just financial advisers

- The benefits to attendees of your seminars

- How to plan, prepare, market and host your seminars

- The special presentation skills needed to deliver your business messages with power, clarity, confidence, conviction and impact

- How to follow up afterwards

- Extra ideas to help maximise profits

For those prepared to master the skills and 'get on with it', the results can be astonishing.

It's important too that financial advisers reading this book don't get hung up on the phrase 'Seminar Selling'. Clearly the profession has moved on from selling products, but like it or not you are selling something – be it your expertise, experience, reputation, credibility or service. For the purposes of this book, 'Seminar Selling' means any activity where you have the opportunity to stand up, present and highlight your expertise, which in turn could result in you attracting new clients.

In fact, businesspeople who do use seminars as part of their sales strategy generally swear by the approach. Andrew Brown is a financial planner in Weston-super-Mare in the UK and is one of those people. I am extremely grateful to him for his fantastic contribution.

Seminar Selling is all about getting on your feet and demonstrating your expertise – live! It's up close and personal and the audience can see the whites of your eyes. It takes guts, hard work, passion, energy and commitment. But get it right and you will never look back. This book removes much of the hard work by revealing everything you need to know to successfully plan, prepare and host your seminars – including the special presentation skills needed to get your business message across with clarity, confidence and conviction.

And here's even better news…

The advent of the internet, social media and new communication technology now provides the opportunity to not only promote your seminars, but to integrate them into your sales and service proposition in a way that will skyrocket your profits. Seminar Selling today is about the skilful combination of a variety of traditional and modern sales and marketing techniques and I hope this book will empower you to discover an exciting, creative, proactive and incredibly profitable new direction for your business.

Throughout the book I refer to 'your seminars' or 'your workshops', which to some readers might imply a formal, intellectual meeting, debate or discussion. I use these words to generically mean *any public event* which you might put on to demonstrate an aspect of business, service or expertise – regardless of the nature of your business. It could be a wine tasting, a craft demonstration or a workshop on how to plan for your retirement. Whatever it is, this book will give you exciting new ideas on how to promote your business more effectively than ever before.

Whilst this book is aimed at financial advisers, at various points throughout the text I have included examples from a range of other industries, businesses and professions, because this helps to remove any blinkers we might be wearing and so see the benefits of hosting seminars from a variety of perspectives.

Also revealed in the book are a number of fantastic marketing tips, tricks and secrets which I have picked up over the years. Some work for me and others don't, but I wanted to include everything that could potentially be of value to the reader. Where I know the source of a particular idea, I have included it. There are others though, which I have attempted to source, but which unfortunately remain part of sales and marketing folklore. If you know the source of any references, please let me know.

How this Book came about

Back in 1991 I had just started work as a Broker Consultant/Account Manager for Zurich Life – a global insurance company.

My job was to highlight and promote our products to independent financial advisers in the City of London and encourage them to recommend them to their clients. In effect we were the wholesalers of products such as life assurance, replacement income insurance, critical illness insurance and a few others. The financial advisers were the retailers, and who would recommend products to their clients not just from Zurich Life, but almost the entire marketplace.

For the most part, our products were high quality and well-priced, and our service was about average compared to others in the same industry. My colleagues and I 'on the road' were well trained in sales and presentation skills, and for the most part it was an enjoyable job. I was targeted with having twenty face-to-face meetings per week with local financial advisers.

However, because I worked in the City, I rarely had need for my company car, as I walked between meetings with financial advisers. This was very enjoyable in the Summer months, but hell in the Winter.

During the Winter, venturing out onto the streets was not so much fun and inevitably my sales figures would take a dip. In the Summer, it was much more appealing being outside, so I usually had more meetings – resulting in my sales figures going back up. It seemed that it was a bit of a numbers game.

One particularly cold and wet February morning I was soaked to the skin and got wondering if there was another way of doing this – perhaps I could telephone the financial advisers rather than go and see them.

But after chatting to a couple of friends who worked for other insurance companies in a similar role, I decided that instead of me going to meet the financial advisers in their offices, I would invite them to come to mine.

After all, the Zurich Building at the end of Fenchurch Street in the City was exceptionally spacious, and within its walls housed several senior executives – including a senior underwriter, a fund manager, the Head of National Accounts and the Chief Executive.

I hatched a plan to start hosting breakfast meetings and occasional workshops for up to twenty financial advisers at a time, where I would wheel out one of the senior managers to give an inspiring talk on some aspect of interest to the financial advice community. All I needed to do was to fill the room, take coats and pour coffee.

The workshops went surprisingly well. I managed to stay dry and warm, the financial advisers were entertained and educated, and my boss commented on my initiative.

I also discovered the amazing power of the free bacon roll to get bums on seats.

It didn't take very long for me to go from seeing up to twenty financial advisers a week, to sometimes seeing twenty *per day*.

And as a result, my sales figures went through the roof, I qualified for all the sales conventions and I eventually got promoted.

I had discovered the startling power of Seminar Selling and Live Marketing.

This book breaks down the benefits of hosting seminars, workshops and simple live marketing events; reveals how to fill the room, shows you how to present your message like a rock star and how to generate high additional profits from your events.

If, as you read this book you feel inclined to ask a question or post about it on Twitter, LinkedIn or your social platform of choice, please use the hashtag #SeminarSelling and I'll do my best to respond. My Twitter handle is @PhilipCalvert and you can find me on LinkedIn at www.linkedin.com/in/saleskeynotespeaker.

Part 1

Successful Seminar Selling:
How to Plan, Prepare and Market Your Events

Problems Facing Small Businesses

Change is a wonderful thing. It keeps life fresh and exciting and brings a wealth of opportunity for anyone who is prepared to grasp it. *'You're either on the train – or under it'* as a colleague once helpfully advised me.

On the other hand, a great many businesspeople don't see it that way. Change brings fear, worry, uncertainty and indecision, which isn't surprising if you are to believe the business editorials of the weekend press, each proclaiming the results of survey after survey on the worries of small businesses. In fact, you would be forgiven for wondering why anyone actually starts their own business.

Survey after survey confirm the current main concerns. These include:

- Brexit
- The potential impact of artificial intelligence
- The changing economic climate
- Cash flow/late payment of bills
- Changing regulations
- GDPR and compliant use of data
- Lack of skilled workers
- The minimum wage
- Competition from overseas
- The overall tax burden
- Getting to grips with ever evolving marketing technologies
- Changing exchange rates
- Cost of transport
- Toxic politics

- Postal problems
- Adapting to new payment technologies

…and so on.

Financial advisers can add a multitude of other concerns that they are all too familiar with, not least of which include compliance, professional indemnity, recruitment, ambulance chasers, the cost of funding the Financial Services Compensation Scheme – and so on.

So clearly, the small business owner does have much to contend with on a day-to-day basis. And one thing is for certain; change will continue for many years to come. Not only will it continue, but it will *confuse* as it continues. Take marketing for example:

Changing technology now gives the small business owner an extraordinary array of promotional tools and methodologies. Here are just a few:

- Telesales
- Face to face sales
- Direct mail
- TV advertising
- Radio advertising
- Newspaper advertising
- Magazine advertising
- Social media and internet marketing
- Funnels
- Podcasting
- Blogging
- Vlogging
- Affinity marketing
- Email marketing

- Key account management
- Relationship management
- SMS messaging
- Virtual and augmented reality

…and many more.

And as we'll discover later – yes, even advertising on the side of sheep!

So surely the degree to which we can adapt to change will determine our ability to profit from it and is key to moving forward in our business. Unfortunately, in the UK we are often slow in recognising when change has happened and by the time we have decided to take advantage of, say, some new technological advance, many of the potential new benefits have often been lost.

As we will see shortly, many small businesses are still not fully embracing the internet regularly to build sales. Most *think* they are, but believe me, they're not! Simply having a website does not necessarily mean we are maximising the potential from e-commerce. For example, I see this time and time again amongst financial advisers, where in my own experience, huge numbers of business owners don't even know their website statistics.

They don't even know the most basic of information such as:

- How many people visited their site last month/week
- How many pages they visited
- Which pages they visited
- How long they stuck around
- Their location

- Search terms used on Google, Bing etc.
- Page they left their site
- Bounce rate

It would be unfair to suggest that all small businesses are internet agnostic. Indeed, since I first wrote this book in 2003, business has been transformed by the internet, with many fortunes having been created *because* of the internet. Yes, people really do make money in their sleep without the need for any human interaction – even at micro-business level. People of all ages now have the opportunity to take advantage of e-commerce opportunities and can set up an internet business at the drop of a hat.

Some financial advisers may feel that their business sector is not appropriate for online sales and that's fair enough, but later on I will show other ways in which you can use your website to generate substantial new sales.

So how does the average business owner look beyond all the distractions of change, Brexit, exchange rates, stealth taxes and late payments and get focused on attracting volume, profitable new clients?

When I ask businesses this question, time and time again their answer has its roots in marketing and lead generation.

One of my target markets is financial planners and advisers, and over the last four decades, lead generation has been their number one cause for concern.

But aligned to lead generation, also comes something else which they deem to be central to survival and growth – and that is their own business' capabilities, i.e. the strength and robustness of their core service proposition.

You can be awesome at marketing, but if you don't have a product and service that is actually relevant in today's world, then you'll soon disappear.

In the example of financial advisers, relevance is becoming more and more important due to the arrival and growth of online services that can essentially replace financial advisers – not to mention estate agents, accountants, travel agents and even retail. No-one is immune to the potential impact of digital disruption.

Businesses that will survive and thrive will be those that are nimble on their feet, forward-thinking and ready and able to adapt what they already do for the new economy.

Unfortunately, many businesses of all sizes fail to do this. Only this week, travel giant Thomas Cook Group plc went into liquidation, with many industry experts citing that they never really kept up to date with new trends in the travel industry. We can all think of countless other large firms in the same boat.

But small businesses, even at micro level need to stay alert to both the potential for disruption and opportunities that are available. And whilst online news, blogs and social media can keep us up to date on new technology developments, it is well worth considering having a non-executive digital director, or business adviser to keep us up to speed on developments which could impact us positively or negatively down the road.

Many small businesses have a tendency to look positively on just about all aspects of new internet technology, because for the most part, the news is generally exciting and good. Though on the downside, 'shiny object syndrome' is very real, and can often lead to a lack of focus and strategic planning in our businesses.

That aside, all small businesses should be alert to technology advances and have (or employ) a trusted adviser who can update us, challenge us and potentially guide us in how we respond to new developments.

And then there's the problem of funding.

Funding for Growth

Funding any growth programme is inevitably going to be a challenge for all small businesses and whilst there are government initiatives, grants and routes to finance available, these resources are not without limit. A clear majority of small businesses resort to bank overdrafts and loans to sustain and grow their organisations, but it's exciting to see the growth of crowd funding as a viable alternative.

How then is it possible for a small business (or any other business for that matter) to respond positively to change, engage proactively in new ventures, increase turnover, improve marketing *and* achieve significant growth all at the same time and without breaking the bank?

A tough question for any business, let alone firms that operate within sectors that are undergoing *additional* change and consolidation as a direct result of technology.

Many commentators now suggest that technology and artificial intelligence will revolutionise everything – and this may well be the case. But in the meantime, there are ways it can be used to support other initiatives which will themselves produce high levels of new business, and we will explore some of these later in this book.

Furthermore, there are some basic sales and marketing issues that are vital to business survival and growth. With everything else to think about, it's easy to forget them:

- You need a regular supply of new and returning clients

- These clients need to trust you

- You need to understand them intimately – this includes understanding their problems

- You need a product or service that solves these problems (more on what I mean by 'product' later)

- You need a service proposition that gives prospects and clients more than they are expecting. This means treating them in ways that will make them loyal customers for life and not treating them how you *think* they want to be treated or how you think they *should* be treated

- Potential clients need evidence of your expertise and, ideally third-party endorsement of your service

- Once potential clients have found you, they must find your product or service *irresistible*

- You need to do it all profitably

Boiled down further these sales and marketing 'business basics' equate to a need for:

- Proactive marketing
- Exceptional creativity skills
- An extremely thorough understanding of clients' needs
- Credibility in business
- The provision of considerable 'added value' through outstanding customer service

In the next chapter we will look at the one and only way that small businesses can incorporate all these 'business basics' within their marketing strategy, proactively move forward whilst increasing sales and profits *and* all within the context of a dramatically changing and often highly regulated business environment.

An impossible dream? Read on.

The Need to Change and Adapt

"The most important thing a small business can do is be clear about what their end game is, be specific about the target market and then prepare a marketing plan covering at least 12 months' activity.

The marketing plan should explore different marketing approaches from direct response mailings, advertising, PR and affinity relationships. They must set up a program of measuring every return from every campaign so that the most effective marketing strategy can be identified. Once they have found something that works, then they should keep on using the approach until it begins to falter. Once this happens, they need to try again with a different approach.

The marketing message must always be benefit driven and focused on the end user and not the business. No one is interested about how great I think my business is – all I want to know is how you are going to help me. WIIFM (What's in it for me?) is all a target cares about.

Having started the marketing process it is vital that you stick with it. Far too often a novice will expect immediate returns from their marketing effort – it never happens.

Keep refining the marketing messages (from the prospect's perspective), test different headlines that grab the attention, make sure that the headline claims are substantiated in the text, explain how the client will benefit if they use your service or buy your product and also what they will lose out on if they don't.

Have a powerful call to action and offer some sort of guarantee that ensures the client will never lose out if they find that the product is not what they want. (Risk reversal is powerful so long as you are confident in your product or service). Finally, use special offers to grab the attention and heighten the sense of loss if they fail to take action."

Roland Rawicz-Szczerbo, formerly Director, Quay Software Solutions Limited (now Director and owner of Time4Advice Ltd)

Any small business owner wishing or needing to proactively move forward, with a view to dramatically increasing sales, requires a great deal of self-motivation and courage – not to mention creative and lateral thinking.

Even if you are an expert in a particular field and have produced a good living from your business, it is very easy to become blinkered in your approach to sales and marketing. If a particular sales approach has worked well enough up until now, then why bother to change it? But is that what you really want?

Ask yourself a few questions:

- Is your current sales and marketing approach producing sufficient *new and profitable* business for you?
- Is it maximising full sales potential?
- Are you over-reliant on referrals?
- Would you like to be selling *more* of your product or service?

- Do you run the risk of this method running out of steam in time?
- Have you thought about new ways of increasing sales to meet the changing needs of clients?

Whatever your answers to these questions, it is vital that you still keep an open mind to a wide variety of new ways of building sales – even if you truly believe you have found the one and only way for your business. Ask yourself this: Is it possible that there might be a better, more sufficient and more cost-effective ways of promoting your financial advice or financial planning service?

My challenge and bet with you is that there is.

Thinking Laterally

First of all, let's explore lateral thinking a bit more. Much has been written about the need for lateral thinking and I don't intend to add a great deal more here. But what is often forgotten is just how hard it is to think laterally.

"Think laterally" we are told on one course after another, as if by magic we can suddenly conjure up exciting new ways to achieve our goals. It just doesn't work like that. What *is* possible though is for business owners to be much more open minded about how they approach problems and opportunities. In businesses of all sizes, we are not very good at this.

"We tried that five years ago and it didn't work (so it won't work now)."

"Clients don't buy our sort of products off the internet."

"Radio advertising wouldn't be right for us."

"We're not salespeople – we provide advice."

You know the sort of thing.

As a result, we stick to the same ways of doing things in the vain hope that business will improve on its own accord and our minds remain firmly closed to new opportunities and new ways of promoting and delivering our products and services.

In Financial Services I have seen this time and time again. If I had a pound for every financial planner who has told me that *"...social media has no place in the world of financial advice"* I could retire now. Yet, when social media is used carefully as part of a well thought-through marketing and communications strategy, it can be incredibly effective.

Try this little test to see if you are thinking laterally:

Write down the next four numbers in this sequence. (If you can get the next six, give yourself a pat on the back!)

3 1 2 8 3 1 3 0...

Unless you can see the answer straight away, I bet that you have approached the problem in much the same way that you always have – by looking for some sort of mathematical formula or pattern.

Memories of school maths lessons come flooding back as your mind searches for the link between each number. And that is, of course, the issue. We're approaching the problem in exactly the same way that we always have.

Wouldn't it be great if we had the ability to 'think laterally' at the switch of a button?!

Now look at the numbers again but open your mind to different possibilities and solutions. You'll see that I've arranged them slightly differently this time to help you…

3 1 2 8 3 1 3 0…

That's enough clues. If you think you know the answer, send an email to me at philip@philipcalvert.com

One way that we could open our minds just a little bit would be to not make assumptions about how clients and prospects want to receive information or use technology.

For example, there is a perception amongst many people that the Internet is not likely to be used to any great extent by 'older people'. Not only is it used, but research paper after research paper says that the internet has a positive impact on their lives, including being able to:

- Contact family and friends around the world (incl, Skype, Messenger. FaceTime, WhatsApp etc.)
- Investigate websites about hobbies and interests
- Manage their bank account
- Research and book flights and holidays
- Check the news
- Search for information on personal finance issues
- Search for local information
- Research family history
- Purchase products
- Read and listen to books
- Watch re-runs of TV programmes

Given information like this, isn't it about time we started to take notice of reports that the so-called 'grey market' is growing at an astonishing rate and shouldn't we now be updating our perception of how older consumers like to obtain information?

I enjoy challenging representatives from different industries who feel that their particular sector is quite advanced in its use of technology. Indeed, many are very advanced when it comes to technology for operational purposes, but often still have a long way to go to make full use of the potential it offers to increase sales.

"Do you think that independent financial advisers (IFAs) are ready for podcasting?" I asked an industry marketing figure about three years ago.

"Not quite" came the rather respectful reply. Again making an assumption based on perception rather than fact. Little did he know that on November 17th 2012, financial planner Pete Matthew from Cornwall had launched the first of what was to be an astonishing run of personal finance podcasts.

As at October 2019, Pete has recorded 399 episodes and seen just shy of three million downloads. In his own words:

"In the last four weeks, 30 (yep, three-zero) new perfect clients have approached Jacksons thanks to the MeaningfulMoney Podcast. It's like someone has turned the tap up to max. I'm now loading clients up into the New Year"

In conclusion, I firmly believe that as businesspeople we make far too many assumptions about how clients and customers want to receive information and spend too little time investigating new ways of making our sales and marketing efforts more innovative or efficient. As a result, we are missing out on huge new opportunities, both at home and abroad.

To some extent this is understandable, perhaps for no other reason than the fact that if our current sales and marketing methodology isn't apparently broken, then there's no need to fix it.

Fear of change and fear that a new approach won't work is a natural inhibiting factor for most businesses. So, wouldn't it be great if we could find an approach to sales and marketing which is not only tried, tested and proven, but also new, profitable, exciting, creative and innovative for most small businesses?

The Benefits of Seminar Selling

"A good idea is not enough to make a business work. Successful entrepreneurs have a knack for exploiting ideas and turning them into commercial reality.

Make sure you have identified a market need and that they are aware of your solution. Without promotion, no one will know your idea exists."

Digby Jones, former Director-General,
Confederation of British Industry (CBI)

Remember our 'business basics' from the first chapter? Here's a quick reminder:

- You need regular communication with both new and existing clients – and they need to trust you.

- You need to understand them and their problems intimately and have a product or service which solves these problems.

- You need a service proposition that gives prospects and clients more than they expect. This means treating them in ways that will make them loyal customers for life and not treating them how you *think* they want to be treated or how you think they *should* be treated.

- Potential clients need evidence of your expertise and, ideally, third party endorsements of your product/service. Once you are in contact with potential clients, they must find your product and service irresistible.

- You need to do it all profitably.

In my view, Seminar Selling is the only real way of promoting your product and service in a way that encapsulates all of these business basics at the same time *and* which enables small businesses on a tight marketing budget to achieve significant increase in sales and profitable growth.

There is a perception though, that Seminar Selling is just for white-collar businesses, so it is important to stress at this point that virtually *any small business* can profit significantly – particularly if you have products or services that benefit from demonstration to explain how they work. In fact, it may well be the case that your product or service may gain more than you realise from a live demonstration.

What is Seminar Selling?

Earl Tupper's plastic consumer products were a revolution in the kitchen when they were first introduced in 1946.

But despite their many advantages, they did not sell very well in retail outlets. So it was decided that the unique advantages of the plastic containers needed demonstrating to help consumers to understand how they worked and to appreciate the key benefits.

The first Tupperware Home Party was held in 1948 with the demonstrations proving incredibly successful – so much so that in 1951, Tupperware products were removed from retail outlets.

The rest, as they say, is history and apparently a Tupperware party takes place somewhere in the world every 2.5 seconds.

But it is interesting to note how the company has adapted and modified its sales approach to cater for changes in society and shopping preferences.

In 1992, the company introduced Custom Kitchen Planning demonstrations where customers could learn about food preparation, microwave cooking and ways to save money on their grocery bills.

Today, the company is making full use of the internet, yet still also uses demonstrations and showcases in shopping centres. Social media too has added to their reach, with multiple country accounts for Tupperware on Instagram. #Tupperware has seen 2.4 million posts and there are multiple permutations on the Tupperware hashtag.

One of their promotional videos on YouTube has heavy focus on the ability to 'party anywhere', including Facebook live streams. And with our ever-increasing interest in healthy eating, the company's marketing goes from strength to strength.

In short, Tupperware are superb exponents of Live Marketing, Seminar or Workshop Selling.

Most of us have attended a seminar, workshop or demonstration at some stage in our lives. Our prime motivation was probably to obtain information on a subject in which we had an interest. It could have been a hobby, or perhaps we wanted more detailed information on a product or service prior to making a major purchase.

We may even have attended a 'party selling' event promoting anything from kitchenware, lingerie, jewellery, water purification products, adult products, security systems, diet plans, scented candles, cleaning products, cosmetics, children's books or crafts. I've even seen stun gun Tasers being promoted at house parties!

And on occasion we will have been given an incentive to attend, with everything from a prize draw, an Amazon voucher, free flights, a mountain bike - through to a wide screen television or maybe £10,000 cash!

But for the most part, it was the *content* of the seminar or workshop that was the influencing factor, and which had the potential to further boost our interest in a subject, product or service. And that is the secret of successful Seminar Selling – *the ability to inspire attendees to come back for more – much more.*

We could just as easily have requested a brochure from the company concerned, or perhaps looked at their website. We could even have asked for a representative to come to our house, but a seminar is different.

Not only are we able to gain much more information than through a brochure or a website, but it gives us an insight into the workings and culture of the company and its people, affording us a glimpse 'behind the scenes' prior to committing ourselves further. And some products simply sell better from the benefit of a demonstration.

As I explained earlier, Seminar Selling encapsulates all our business basics, giving us a platform to promote and demonstrate the services of our business and allows potential clients to see and experience us and our product in a 'live' and fun environment without pressure, thus enabling a relationship and trust to develop.

Your seminar or event can be anything from a full day, flashy, professional, multi-media presentation in a smart hotel or conference venue to a simple 'how to' demonstration or workshop in your shop, office premises or home.

Without realising it, you may already give demonstrations to potential clients and there's a good chance that you yourself have been influenced to make purchases as a result of seeing a demonstration.

It happens everywhere without you even noticing – for example, department stores that give cosmetic and make-up demonstrations; wine merchants and off-licences offering free tastings; kitchen and houseware demonstrations at county fairs.

The purpose of this book is to show you how to harness the considerable benefits of promoting your products and services at seminars and workshops and to give you the confidence and skills to transfer these benefits to your own business.

How Seminar Selling works

I witnessed a superb example of this when I was speaking at a Women in Enterprise event in South Wales, where a young lady (Nadine) was welcomed as a new member to the group. Without realising she had done it, Nadine provided the best possible example of Live Marketing and Seminar Selling in action.

Nadine was in the process of starting her new business as a Colour and Image Consultant, showing clients - predominantly women - how to discover and enhance the best aspects of their appearance and how to choose clothing and accessories of the correct colour for their skin and hair tones. During her ten-minute presentation to introduce herself (her first ever 'stand up' presentation) she demonstrated her colour analysis technique by holding swatches of different coloured material under the faces of two female volunteers from the audience.

It was clear to anyone that volunteer number one was in need of a rethink in her choice of wardrobe, whilst volunteer number two could possibly benefit by wearing darker shades of browns and greens. I must admit to having found the experience fascinating and would, given sufficient time, have been curious to find out if my own choice of a dark blue pin-stripe suit, white shirt and red tie was 'doing it' for me – and the audience.

And then came the best part. When Nadine sat down after her ten minutes, there followed a coffee break, and during that time virtually every woman present gave Nadine a business card and requested either further information or an appointment.

In that ten-minute presentation, Nadine acquired two hundred new leads. Hot leads at that.

What Nadine achieved in just ten minutes is what this book is all about. Yes, she was going to produce leaflets, brochures and build a website, but there was nothing to beat the power of her presentation or the amazingly effective live demonstration of her service. Quite simply, Nadine's mini workshop inspired the audience and they wanted more.

Doubtless you can now think of other examples of Seminar Selling:

- The wine importer who offers wine appreciation lessons

- The florist who gives flower arranging workshops in her shop

- The hairdresser who demonstrates how to achieve different cuts and styles

- The firm of accountants that run workshops on how to minimise tax

- The financial adviser who holds retirement and pension planning seminars

- The music shop that gives guitar and instrument demonstrations

- The book shop that gives late night readings

- The presentation skills coach who holds speech workshops for grooms, fathers of the bride and best man

- The vets who run workshops on pet care for children and their parents

- The antique dealers who run workshops on how to value china, glass and furniture

- The restaurant owner who offers cookery classes

- The broker who runs mortgage workshops for first time-buyers

- The interior designers who demonstrate how to make your home more attractive prior to putting it up for sale

And so on.

Take a moment now to think of a creative way you could promote your own financial advice business at either a seminar or workshop. Write down three ideas to demonstrate your product, service or expertise that would be of real benefit to existing or potential clients:

1.

2.

3.

Another great example of Seminar Selling at its finest was when Black & Decker were looking for ways to make its excellent power tools look more attractive to the professional builder and not just the DIY enthusiast.

Their new professional brand was DeWALT, a name synonymous with great quality, strength, performance and power. But it was no good just telling potential customers how good the tools were – they needed people to *see, try and experience them* for themselves.

So in 2002 the company embarked on a massive campaign of live outdoor demonstrations where builders could come from far and wide to see and try the tools. They could cut things in half, drill holes, nail things together and hammer and saw to their hearts' content. They even ran the Million Dollar Challenge – an incredible nationwide competition where builders, contractors and power tool enthusiasts compete in regional heats to win a million dollars.

All they had to do was sink five screws into a piece of wood in the shortest possible time. There were over 400 qualifying events across the United States and Canada to find just 14 finalists who would compete for one million dollars.

The 2002 winner ('King of the Drill') was Jon Smith, a general contractor from Delaware, Ohio who drove five screws in a very respectable 6.77 seconds. Well done Jon!

The 2003 heats had over 500 special events staged for over 100,000 competitors. Specially fitted Million Dollar Vehicles visited power tool retailers, construction sites and home centres where, according to the DeWALT website, people 'can test their prowess driving screws with a cordless drill'.

Great fun. And if you missed the action, you can see video clips on YouTube. I wonder which brand of power tools Jon and all the other contestants will be using for the rest of their lives…?

So we can see that although there have been incredible advances in communication technology, it is the high-visibility, high-touch approach which really hits the spot.

The Benefits of Seminar Selling and Live Marketing to Financial Advisers

From what you have read already, you are hopefully already getting a sense for how powerful this approach can be. And when an event is combined with social media, video and other communication technology, the overall impact of your event can be considerable.

Let's get under the hood:

- Potential clients get to *see and experience* you, your product and your service in action, before they make a purchase

- Just holding the event at all positions you as an expert on the subject concerned – if not *the* expert. And the simple act of standing and using visuals as part of a sales related activity can increase the amount prospects are prepared to spend by about 25%!

- Seminar Selling is incredibly cost effective. Even if you don't charge a fee for attendance, consider your current cost of acquiring a client and compare it to the cost of having a room full of warm customers. The fact that they have turned up at all makes them a warm lead by definition, so you have multiple prospects all present at the same time

- Seminar Selling is even more cost effective if you charge an entry fee. In fact, if you do, your delegates or attendees are paying to be your prospects! We will explore the pros and cons of charging an entry fee in chapter 4

- Hosting a seminar or workshop gives you the opportunity to promote additional products and services, thus making the event even more profitable. More on this in chapter 7

- Speaking to a room full of people and *just demonstrating your expertise* actually takes the pressure off you, as you are not overtly trying to sell your product or service. I repeat, seminars are a demonstration of your expertise and the chance for people to see what you do 'live', so there is no need to make a blatant sales pitch for business

- Seminars enable people to form a more detailed and valued opinion about you. This helps them to build trust without having to speak to you. They can also look at the reactions of other people in the audience and gauge how they too are responding

- Conversion rates at seminars can be extremely high. By conversion rates, I mean people who approach you later with a view to purchasing your main product or service, or who approach you for a personal consultation based on your expertise.

Andrew Brown, a financial adviser based in the South West of England wrote to me:

"*(Our) seminars would typically be attended between 35-55 people, and the conversion rate was always extremely high and often approaching 100%.*"

Enough said…

- Of those attendees who do not subsequently approach you, you have at least warmed them up for another day. A key skill in Seminar Selling is relationship building, so that even if they are not ready to make a purchase now, they may wish to in the future. We will show you how to do this with your presentation later on.

- Holding a seminar or workshop can massively increase your list of contacts for your newsletter. Regular communication with clients or potential clients is essential for any small business and a newsletter is an ideal way of doing this. Ideally, I would recommend an email newsletter and in Chapter 6 we'll show you how to use email newsletters to support your business, support your seminars, drive people to your website and increase sales.

    That said, do not discount the idea of also sending out a high quality *paper* newsletter. Martin Bamford, a very tech-savvy financial adviser in Cranleigh, UK produces an excellent and high-quality paper version of his email newsletter, which is very well received by his clients. And if you produce a paper newsletter, it makes a great giveaway to attendees of your seminar or live events. More on 'back of room' products later.

- Some people find that after holding a few seminars or workshops, new doors unexpectedly start to open for them. It is possible to get very well known in a particular field and consequently be in demand as an expert speaker on your subject. Some people even find their seminars are so successful that their presentation becomes more in demand than their main product or service. This also can lead to more speaking work, private consultations and consequently the need to completely re-engineer their business.

- Seminars and live marketing events are a great way to raise and enhance your profile locally. Martin Bamford who I mentioned a moment ago, told me that he has attracted new clients from people who did *not* attend his seminar because they couldn't make it, but just seeing the promotions for his event was enough to persuade them to make contact with him.

The Benefits of Seminars to Attendees

It goes without saying that the benefits of such events work both ways, and whilst they are a proven marketing tool for the business owner, they are also hugely valuable and beneficial to attendees. So in putting our events together, we need to play to these benefits.

- The most important benefit of seminars or workshops to attendees is that your event enables them to build up a picture for themselves of the quality of your product or service and the nature of your expertise. Rather than rely on a third party's recommendation, they can judge for themselves if your service is right for them – either now or in the future. Your presentation is, for them, the living embodiment of your business and the perception they build will be all that matters.

- Any business that relies heavily on a service-based proposition needs to build a relationship with its clients. Equally, clients need to have a relationship with your business and seminars provide an excellent opportunity for people to get to know a business before moving to the next stage of your value ladder – be it a personal consultation or to make their purchase.

- Different people like to receive information in different ways. Many business owners wrongly make assumptions about how clients and prospects will want to receive information about their product or service – often because they have never actually asked them how they would like to be communicated with.

> Unless you know exactly how your clients like to receive information, offer it in a variety of formats. One of the most under used is the seminar format, where people can engage many more senses – thus increasing the likelihood of your message being remembered and acted upon.

Former Nutritionist of the Year and motivational speaker Trish Tucker May provides a good example.

When I first met her almost twenty years ago, Trish talked about how businesspeople can increase passion, energy and enthusiasm for their work and thus revitalise themselves and their business.

As part of her excellent presentation, she gave everyone in the audience a taste of her *Passion Potion* – a deep pink, healthy juice drink with a secret ingredient!

Quite apart from the quality and content of her message, by giving everyone a taste of the Passion Potion, she was not only engaging with people's senses of sight and sound, but also touch, taste and smell – not to mention their imaginations!

Trish is based in Australia, and has further developed her healthy lifestyle business, using workshops at the heart of her promotions. Not only do these market her services, but also create an income stream in their own right.

Let me repeat that last sentence because it is incredibly important going forward:

'Not only do these market her services, but also create an income stream in their own right.'

Trish's workshops are also fun and entertaining and naturally create loyal advocates for her business. Her range of workshops include:

- Over 50 and Feeling Fabulous
- Better sleep, more energy, less overwhelm
- Healthy, happy kids
- Women's wellness days
- Fermentation and juicing for beginners
- Detox your home
- Introduction to natural healing and essential oils

What workshops could *you* create around your service and expertise as a financial planner?

It's really important that you don't make assumptions about *why* people attend seminars. Stimulating as your presentation may be, there are some people who come along just for the lunch or the 'freebies'. Remember my bacon roll from earlier...?

Yes, there are always a few like this in every audience and you'll find plenty at exhibitions and trade shows! If you do take a stand at these events, make sure that you have attractive carrier bags made up with your company name and website address, so that people have something in which to carry all their freebies. But make sure that *your* carrier bags are the largest as you will find that people put all the other bags they collect inside the largest. Yours needs to be on the *outside*!

But... freebies are an important aspect of attracting people to your event in your marketing materials, and we'll get to this in detail later. Essentially, a free gift is part of your package of incentives for people to attend.

But some people attend seminars, workshops and live marketing events simply because they know that there will be other people there with whom they share something in common. And this is a key ingredient to consider when promoting your events.

Networking

There are many people who attend seminars or workshops purely for the networking opportunity. By networking, you are not only finding potential new business contacts, but you are also, in effect, promoting yourself in the subtlest of ways – a more subtle form of live marketing.

Don't underestimate the importance of the networking aspect for attendees. It is a vital part of business and social lives – regardless of age. So encourage attendees to network to their hearts' content during the various breaks.

In fact, highlight it by including it in your promotional material as one of the benefits of attending your seminar e.g. *superb networking opportunity!*

In the United States (where it is estimated that there are approximately 20,000 seminars every day) they see the networking aspect as one of the key benefits of attending.

But for 'networking', also read 'social warmth'. Even if your event is not aimed at businesspeople, the ability to be with other people where you share something in common, is a key draw to live events.

The Keys to Success

So it can be seen that the benefits of promoting your services in a live environment are considerable. Personally, I think the keys to the success of Seminar Selling are threefold:

First, there is the aspect of clarity.

Attendees are given an opportunity to see you and/or your product/service in action – warts and all – and this gives them the chance to get answers to the questions they want clarity on.

There are sadly far too many consumers out there who simply don't understand what a financial adviser does – and our entire industry/profession must take responsibility for that. Over many years, we have frankly made an appalling job of promoting and marketing the great work that the financial advice community does, so a seminar helps to clear the fog of misunderstanding.

Second, by seeing you or your service in action, they are able to 'try before they buy' or put a toe in the water prior to committing themselves further.

Third, there is the social aspect.

By sitting anonymously in an audience of people, attendees can observe other people's reactions to the seminar host, they can network for new business contacts and the social warmth of a gathering with likeminded people helps to oil the wheels of the sales cycle.

But despite the considerable benefits of this sales approach, many businesspeople resist holding seminars. There are natural concerns about the amount of planning involved and the lack of experience in marketing such events. Over the next two chapters we look at how to plan your seminars or workshops and how to market them to get 'bums on seats'.

~

"The Million Dollar Challenge accomplished two key strategic objectives for DeWALT.

First, our distribution base looks to us to create events at their stores that generate excitement and provide reasons for their customers to make purchases. By creating a national event with a theme, we were able to stretch tight budgets by getting other manufacturers, such as Chevrolet, Carhartt Clothing, and others to join with us and financially support the event, thereby making the whole promotion bigger than what we could have done on our own.

Second, we increased brand affinity for DeWALT with our key construction end users, who were able to satisfy their desire to compete with skills that they use on their jobs every day. In the end, we awarded the million dollar prize at a NASCAR (National Association for Stock Car Auto Racing) event and our driver won the race that day, making it one of the most exciting days in DeWALT history."

Nolan D. Archibald, Chairman and Chief Executive Officer of The Black & Decker Corporation

Planning Your Seminars and Workshops

"Defining your target is key.

Do your research – think about their lifestyle – where might they go, what else they buy and how they like to buy. Thinking laterally can open up some amazing cost-effective promotional routes.

Once you have your target customer defined, take a critical eye at your sales process, ensuring that at each stage you are meeting or preferably exceeding client expectations. This is nothing ground-breaking, but something that a number of businesses seem to overlook these days.

We take communication with our clients, written or verbal extremely seriously and a bugbear of mine is to be promised a call by Friday and not to receive it. Regardless of whether you have anything to tell your client, if you promised you would call, call!

From the first contact to the final invoice you have countless opportunities to get your brand and what it stands for in front of your client, so make the most of them."

Jacqui Smith, Director, HomeSmiths Ltd

The planning of your event is, surprisingly, a relatively easy part of the process – provided that a few important rules are followed closely.

A key objective of the planning process is to 'get bums on seats' and Chapter 5 will examine the best way to go about marketing and promoting your events.

In this chapter, we look at everything else you need to do to make sure your seminar or workshop is a success and I strongly suggest you follow my 'Rule of Five'.

> 5 months + 5 decisions + 5 planning stages = successful seminar selling

When do I start planning my seminar?

The most important piece of advice I can give in this book is not to underestimate the amount of time needed to plan and market your seminars.

This is not because there is so much work to do, but more to give you enough time to make sure that what *must* be done, actually gets done.

After all, until seminars become integrated into your day-to-day activities, you still have a business to run and there will probably be greater priorities with which to concern yourself.

Give yourself a full five months to set up your first seminar, after which you should be able to move to a three-month cycle as you learn from your first few events. So, if you want to hold your first seminar on, for example, 13 November, you need to start to work on it on 13 June.

But even in this example you may want to consider starting work earlier because key helpers are likely to be on holiday at some stage during the process.

What are the main decisions that need to be made?

Decision 1 – What are my objectives for the event?

Firstly, you need to have *two* objectives. An objective for yourself, and an objective for your audience.

Your seminars or workshops will fail unless you have a clear objective for what *you* want to achieve. As they say – if you fail to plan, you plan to fail.

Make sure too that you have a separate objective for what you want *the delegates to do* as a result of attending your seminars.

On the surface it sounds like these two objectives will be the same, however there is a subtle difference between what *you* want to achieve and what you want *the attendees to do* as a result of your presentation. The two objectives together will provide a very clear focus for your events.

Here are some examples of objectives for *you*. Do you want to:

- Increase awareness of your company locally or nationally?

- Increase awareness of your services locally (or wider)?

- Attract new clients locally or nationally?

- Enhance your reputation for quality services?

- Enhance your reputation as being the leading experts in your field?

- Draw attention to other services that sell less well?

- Announce new products or services?

- Build relationships and strategic partnerships with other businesses and professional introducers?

- Offer a social event for loyal clients and their friends? (remember 'and their friends' for later.)

- Pass on your expertise to others?

- Prove the worth or effectiveness of your service through demonstration?

- Make money by charging for attendance?

- Try out a new distribution route?

These and others could be objectives for your events and only you will know what is appropriate for your business.

But you *must* have objectives, as they will provide direction for everything you do in the planning and promotional phases.

Next – write them down, keep them visible and refer back to them regularly, particularly on the day of the seminar.

Your objectives will also guide you on the type of event you wish to hold. Here are some suggestions:

- A whole day workshop
- A half day (morning or afternoon) seminar or workshop
- A breakfast meeting
- A lunchtime event
- An evening event
- A weekend boot camp (either at home or abroad) or retreat
- An open day at your place of work with ongoing demonstrations
- A networking or social event
- Industry exhibitions, trade shows and fairs
- Craft fairs and county shows
- A showcase, talk or presentation at business clubs

Try to choose the format that best suits your objectives, your subject matter and the type of person you are targeting.

Decision 2 – What Should be the Subject Matter?

Your subject matter will be guided by your main objective and should focus on what it is that you want people to take away, remember and act upon. And when you think about it, this is crucial. Attendees must act if you are to get the high conversion rates needed to increase profits.

In a later chapter we look at some other ways to decide on content and specific presentation skills which will help people to remember much more of what you tell them and thus increase the likelihood of them being motivated to talk to you in person after the event.

Within the context of your objective, your subject matter should not be too broad or too wide-ranging, as this will lessen its overall appeal.

Generally speaking, the more niche the subject matter, the higher the likely level of interest. That is not to say that a talk or presentation at a generic level won't have appeal, but what will have more appeal is if the generic level is narrowed.

For example, a demonstration on watercolour painting will certainly have appeal to many, but a demonstration on landscape watercolour painting will have greater appeal. Of greater appeal still will be a demonstration on autumn landscape watercolour painting.

Financial advisers should particularly take care not to be too generic in their presentation, as they will inevitably struggle to get bums on seats. Clear focus on a particular financial issue experienced by clients will always have more appeal in your marketing and promotions.

The important thing in all seminars is not to cross over the line to the point where you appear to be selling a product. Successful Seminar Selling is about enhancing the perception of your expertise – not overtly selling.

Feel free to demonstrate your product or service by all means, but make absolutely sure people can see how they would benefit or how it would enhance their lives.

Decision 3 – Who are my Target Audience and how many should attend?

Again, the target audience will be guided by the objective of your event and having a clear target audience will make your promotion easier.

A key question is whether you want an audience full of existing or potential clients.

The answer is of course both.

Existing clients should be more predisposed to attending and, ultimately, are more profitable. New prospects offer the potential to grow your customer base, which in turn should increase further as they refer you to other people over time.

Others you could target include people and businesses who are in a position to introduce business to you – so in the case of financial advisers that would include local estate agents, accountants and solicitors. This infers that a good mix of attendees at a financial adviser's seminar should include:

1. Existing clients
2. People not yet known to you who have responded to your seminar promotions
3. Professional introducers

It's also worth inviting local journalists or influencers in any niche markets that you have. More on this later.

Different types of attendees require a different marketing approach, which we will examine in the next chapter. Whatever your proposed mix of audience members, always consider the potential networking opportunities for them and wherever possible try to get at least a small number of your personal friends to be present. A few friendly faces in the crowd will put you at ease.

How many people should attend?

The more niche your event the fewer will attend, but the greater likelihood of them eventually becoming a client.

Your numbers will also be influenced by the budget you have and your venue. If you are putting on a demonstration in your office premises, clearly it is easier to make a decision on numbers. If you think you have the potential to get 100 people along, then you will need to look at larger venues.

But my main advice here is don't put too much pressure on yourself by going for too big an event too soon.

Whenever I ask people who are thinking about putting on a seminar or live marketing event how many people they would expect to attend, the average answer comes out around fifty. In my view, this is too many if you are still getting started with seminars and client events.

Start smaller. If you aim for (say) ten people, it will be a lot easier to fill the room than when aiming for fifty. And clearly going for a smaller number initially has implications for costs.

Start small, get some experience, note your learning points, build some confidence and then move on to something bigger.

Decision 4 – Should I Charge a Fee for Attendance?

Whilst it is not essential, charging a fee for attendance can make a huge difference in the level of your profits from seminars and has other advantages too. However, many seminar hosts resist charging an entry fee for fear that people will not pay to attend.

This could not be further from the truth and I have seen no evidence to show that a sensible, but worthwhile fee puts off people from attending. Indeed, charging a fee actually *increases their perception of the value of the event* and attendees will be paying to be your prospects! Furthermore, the more niche your market, the higher price you can charge.

How much should I charge?

If we use the example of a whole day workshop as a guide, you can adjust the price accordingly for shorter events. Anything from £75 to £250 appears typical for whole day events across a variety of industries and I personally have charged £147 per ticket, or £97 for early booking.

As an alternative I have charged £127 per ticket for purchases of two or more, or £87 for the equivalent 'early-bird' price. Before we talk about discounts, let's do some quick sums.

Let's take that example of ten people and charge them £127 each. Straight off the bat you have £1,270 towards your costs and you might even make some profit.

Now imagine you're feeling more confident and you get forty people to attend at an early-bird price of £97 and a further ten at the full price of (say) £147.

That's £5,350 in the bank before you've even said a word and will cover the cost of the event many times over.

Now imagine that (let's be generous) 25% of the attendees want to make an appointment with you and eventually purchase your main product or service – you can soon start to see how the profits increase dramatically. Not only is it possible to achieve conversion rates at this level and higher, but in Chapter 7 we'll show you how to multiply these profits many times over.

It's important to also think carefully about the amount you charge, because this changes the perceived value of your event.

For example, let's imagine that you are a high-end financial planner who works with CEOs in medium sized companies who are nearing retirement. You have decided to host a seminar aimed at this market and you come up with two pricing options for a ticket:

£10 per ticket, or
£250 per ticket

Which of the two instinctively feels like the best option to go for if you were a CEO?

Clearly it's the £250 option, because of the perceived value. £10 *looks* appealing – but also cheap – and whilst people in your target market are careful with their money, they don't do cheap.

Your pricing will also be guided by the type of event that you are hosting, the location and value that you propose to include.

I have a collection of examples of great seminar marketing, with one of my favourites being a promotional package from Nido Qubein of a two night/three day 'Wealth Weekend' that he was hosting as far back as 2004. The price? $12,600 – and that didn't include your accommodation.

Perception of value is everything.

Discounts and Incentives

Regardless of whether you are offering a free or chargeable event, we need to remember that everything we include in our promotional materials will move people either towards or away from making the decision to commit and attend.

I call the moment of decision the tipping point, and everything we do in our communications should be designed to move people towards their personal tipping point.

Some people will reach their tipping point quite quickly, whilst others may take a very long time to get there.

Now let's be brutally honest here – it will be extremely unlikely that someone who sees your promotions will open your mailing or email, or see your promotional web page and say:

"Oh, my goodness - I've been waiting for this event all of my life. I'll cancel my forthcoming wedding so that I can attend!"

That's just not going to happen.

Some people will just plain ignore your promotions because it's not for them. But if you have targeted your marketing carefully and used the techniques I'm about to share, you should, at the very least get their attention. And the job of the content of your promotion is to nudge them up to their tipping point when they decide to say "Yes!"

The things that will nudge them to that point are:

- Your hook
- Your story
- Your offer
- Your incentives
- Your discounts (if appropriate)
- Your value stack
- Your copywriting

As we have been discussing whether or not we should charge a fee for attendance, let's start with some focus on manipulating that fee with discounts… And we all love a discount.

I won't deny that charging a fee seems a big step for many potential seminar and workshop hosts, but although the fee itself will enhance the perception of the event's quality and value, it is possible to manipulate the entrance fee in a variety of ways to make it more attractive – and indeed irresistible.

In fact, your discounted price should be your 'real' price, so set your advertised price at a high level but expect people to pay the lower amount, e.g. £97 as opposed to £147 in the example above.

Also offer discounts for:

- Multiple bookings
- Members of the Institute of Directors (IoD)
- Members of the Federation of Small Businesses (FSB)
- Members of local business clubs
- Women in Business Clubs
- Chamber of Commerce
- Round Table
- Export clubs
- Trade associations
- Networking and referral groups e.g. Business Network International (BNI), NRG etc.

If you really know your target market, you will probably have a good idea where else they hang out, so offer discounts for members of:

- The local golf club
- Running club
- Cycling club
- Tennis club
- Bridge club
- …and so on.

One of my favourites is to offer a discount for members of LinkedIn! If you run a Facebook group, offer members a discount.

Offer existing clients/customers a discount too. Offer local introducers a discount.

In addition, you can offer a discount if people quote a special reference number from an advertisement. This also helps you to track which promotional method is most effective.

Some people are still not entirely comfortable booking anything online, so why not offer a discount for booking by text message – or even by post!

Look out too for any subsidies that might be available for training, because these can help to bring down the price of your tickets. There are occasionally national subsidies which have the objective of, amongst other things, improving and developing the skills of employed people, tackling long-term unemployment, improving training opportunities, encouraging entrepreneurship and promoting equal opportunities for women in the workplace.

Some subsidies may be available locally, so approach your local council and universities to see if anything is available.

So in the case of your own seminars and workshops, if your events are deemed to qualify and assist in these aims, some of your attendees may be able to claim a refund of a substantial portion of the price of their ticket. I should say that such subsidies are becoming increasingly difficult to find, but it is worth some investigation.

In my own experience, the combination of **charging an entry fee** and **attendees being able to obtain a discount** is an extremely powerful draw.

On the one hand the entry fee enhances the perception of the value of the event, yet on the other attendees believe they are getting a real bargain if they don't have to pay full price.

Even if your event is not the sort where there is the potential for attendees to receive a subsidy, offer discounts anyway.

As we will see in the next chapter, much of the success of your events will depend on getting bums on seats. A really effective way of doing this is to offer a free ticket for every ticket paid for, or three for the price of two.

Many people feel more comfortable if they attend seminars with a friend or colleague, so make it easier for them to bring someone along by offering them a free ticket with their own. Don't worry if that eats into your profits – you'll discover later how free entrants will soon become profitable!

In short, be as flexible as you can on how people make a booking, how they pay for it and what they pay. If someone wants to book and they don't fall into any discountable categories, **still find a reason to offer them a discount**.

When people call to ask if they qualify or say that they have just missed the early booking discount, tell them you are in a good mood today or the sun is shining or it's your cat's birthday – **just make sure that everyone gets a discount**.

Don't forget, the way you deal with people at this stage tells them a lot about you and your business. Make sure that you come across as friendly, professional and flexible, because for them, the event starts there and then on the phone. Once they have bought into you as a person, they will buy your product or service –guaranteed.

Other Incentives

At the end of the day it is the content of your events which primarily drive the decision as to whether someone will attend or not, because subconsciously they are asking themselves *"What's in it for me?"*

But there are other things you can do to convince people to pay to attend.

1. Offer a full refund in your promotional materials. Offering a full refund if the customer is not completely satisfied with the goods is often seen in shops and stores. There is no reason why you can't do the same if an attendee at your event is not completely satisfied. Offering a full 'no questions asked' refund is almost a challenge to find fault and also shows that you are extremely confident in the quality of your seminar or workshop.

2. Bonus materials. There's a lot of talk in business at the moment about the importance of providing 'added value' to customers. But whatever it is that you provide by way of added value for attending your event, it must be tangible in the eyes of the recipient. It will have even more value to them if they think it is exclusive to them, exclusive to attendees or to the business group of which there are a member.

    We will cover this further in Chapter 5 of this book,

but wherever possible specify to potential attendees the 'extras' that they will receive for attending and try to quantify their value – thus giving the impression that *only* attendees at your event will receive them. This is known as your value stack.

3. Recordings of your event. We are going to talk about this in further detail later, but offering a video or audio recording of the event, usually acts as an excellent incentive for attending.

4. CPD (Continuing Professional Development) points are also a big incentive for people in some industries. If your presentation is accredited for CPD, you should highlight this as another great benefit of attending.

At the very least, any seminar host can provide a simple Certificate of Attendance and it's always a good idea to highlight this amongst your incentives for attending.

Don't forget, even the tiniest thing like a certificate will help nudge people to the tipping point when they decide to commit to attending.

Decision 5 – Location, Date and Time

The location of your event will often be determined by the nature of your business. If you are a florist for example, your own shop premises would be ideal, but you would undoubtedly be restricted by space.

In this situation, a good solution would be to run a regular series of quite short flower arranging demonstrations, each perhaps lasting about 45 minutes to an hour.

Think about who your attendees will be and work out from there when they would be most likely to be able to attend. Of course, there is nothing to stop you from using another venue.

Hotels are the most obvious choice, though unless you go very upmarket, they often lack atmosphere and can be a bit pricey if you're not charging an entry fee. On the plus side, most are geared up for virtually any type of meeting event, have plenty of parking and usually have all the necessary presentation equipment to hand. In addition, refreshments are easily available.

In short, much of the hassle of putting on a seminar or workshop will be taken care of by someone else – but that's what you are paying for. My concern about using hotels is not so much the cost, but that many of the chains are a bit 'samey' and sanitised.

Again, unless you have chosen a fabulous five-star hotel, there will be no curiosity value for attendees, so try to find slightly unusual venues where the setting itself has the potential to offer added value.

Remember what I said earlier about nudging people towards their tipping point? The venue you choose will be one of the factors which helps people to make their decision.

Several years ago, I assisted at a seminar in Knightsbridge in the heart of London. The venue for the event was a private ladies club, which made for extremely elegant surroundings and meticulous attention to detail.

I have also used Denbies Wine Estate in Dorking, Surrey as a seminar venue. Dorking is an old market town some 25 miles south of the centre of London and boasts England's largest vineyard and a magnificent chateau style visitor centre.

When building the centre, they were clearly aware of their potential as a conference venue and include as part of their delegate rate:

- A high-quality buffet lunch.

- A Wine Experience tour of the working winery on a specifically made people mover.

- A special effect 360° film.

- A tasting of their magnificent wines in the atmospheric cellars.

Denbies also has a superb shop where, naturally, the visitor or seminar attendee will not be able to resist making a purchase from a huge range of high-quality goods and wines. As a location for a workshop or seminar, Denbies Wine Estate has much to offer and is likely to be far more attractive as a venue for your attendees than yet another hotel conference room.

And of course, Denbies is in itself a fine example of a business that benefits from Seminar Selling and Live Marketing in more ways than one. After a whole day event I ran at the venue, my delegates went off for their film, tour and tasting and over an hour later they each emerged from the shop clutching several bottles of the local produce. Not only did they enjoy a fine workshop on the benefits of

Seminar Selling, but they also proved the concept worked by patronising the venue itself.

In choosing your venue, you should also consider who you are inviting.

A few years ago, I did some work with a very upmarket firm of financial advisers whose target market was pension schemes and employee benefits packages for medium to large businesses.

The company was expanding, and as part of which was opening an office in Northampton which is close to the centre of England.

The directors decided that to announce their arrival in the area and to start building their profile amongst target businesses, they would hold a seminar – targeting the HR heads of appropriately sized companies. They could have chosen from any number of big name branded hotels in the area, but opted to differentiate and book somewhere special – in this case Althorp – the Grade 1 listed stately home of the Spencer family since 1508. The late Princess Diana is also buried on the estate.

In addition to top quality speakers, the event included a magnificent lunch in the family dining room and a tour. What's more Earl Spencer himself was there in person to welcome guests. As I shook hands with him, he smiled and said, *"Welcome to my home"*. Nice.

Clearly you can see that quite apart from the quality content being presented at the seminar, the venue itself was going to attract many of their target attendees.

You don't have to go as far as hiring a stately home for your events but use your imagination and think carefully about what you could do or venues that you could use that would attract your target attendees.

If you have trouble finding a venue for your events, there are multiple websites and services online that can help you. But wherever you choose, make absolutely sure that it is easy to get to and easy to find...

Do your research:

- Can you get in and set up the night before?

- Is access to your venue hindered by rush hour traffic?

- Is the venue within five minutes of a motorway junction?

- Is the venue within a short drive (or walk) from the railway or underground station?

- Will the venue allow you to pay on the day or after your event?

- Is there access for disabled delegates?

- Does the venue have an attractive website (which includes directions*)?

- Is the room you are using easy to locate at the venue immediately on arrival?

- If you are using several rooms for your seminar (e.g. the breakout sessions etc.), are they all on the same floor of the venue or will people have to move between floors? (This can be a nightmare if your timings are tight.)

- Does the room you are using have plenty of natural daylight?

- Does the room you are using have any annoying pillars that restrict the view?

- Does the air conditioning work properly?

- Is there room for people to stretch their legs at the back should they get uncomfortable during the presentation?

- Is there plenty of (free) parking?

- If a hotel, can you negotiate a discount for people who want to stay overnight?

- Are there any other local attractions, which could add value to your event?

- Can you negotiate a discount with local attractions, which could form part of your marketing?

- Can you get hold of testimonials from previous clients?

A quick point about hotels and directions above*

For some reason I don't understand, many hotel venues do not publish the correct post code. I know this sounds ridiculous in this day and age, but if I had a pound for every time the sat nav has taken me to the wrong place because the post code was incorrect on the venue website...

Check it yourself and do a dry run of your journey, because you want to make everything as easy and as stress free as possible for your guests.

When people arrive at your event you want them to be in a positive, receptive and friendly frame of mind. If they have had to struggle through traffic it will be your fault – not theirs, even if they did get up late.

You should also check that the room you are using is easy to find within the venue, and if not, you should bring along some signage in the form of one or more pull-up banners.

On the day of your event, make a point of speaking to whoever is in charge at the front of house and tell them about your event. Explain how many guests are expected and politely suggest that they are made a fuss of. In the minds of your guests, the event starts the moment they set foot in the venue – and that includes the car park.

Take a leaf out of *Mugaritz* – the internationally acclaimed restaurant in Rentería, Guipúzcoa, Spain. Since 2006 it has been considered one of the world's best restaurants according to Restaurant Magazine and has been ranked fourth on the list.

Quite apart from its food and wines, it is their attention to detail which makes all the difference. It may be a very small point, but when you park your car at Mugaritz, someone comes out to the car park to meet and welcome you. So for guests, the experience begins before they have even set foot in the restaurant.

When putting on your own event, what could you do that surprises and delights people before it even gets started?

When is the best time and date hold seminars?

Again, your type of business, objectives and target audience will often dictate this. If, for example, your event is targeted at people with young families, then clearly the hours of 8am – 9am and between 3pm and 4.30pm are not advisable. Put yourself in their shoes and think carefully about when they are most likely to be able to attend or would want to attend.

If your target audience works during the day think about when the best time would be for them. Could you run a breakfast meeting, or a workshop at lunchtime?

I know of a mortgage broker in Northern Ireland whose target market was first-time buyers, so he held his seminars at 11.30 am on Saturday mornings – the time when most of them were available to attend.

Sometimes though, you can *think* you are doing the right thing by your audience, but circumstances can conspire against you.

One dark February a few years ago, I attended a financial adviser's seminar as a mystery shopper. His head office had asked me to go along as a delegate and report back on how the event went from my perspective.

The quality of the venue was outstanding – a five-star country hotel with comfy armchairs and roaring fires. The theme of the seminar was 'Lifestyle in Retirement' and attendees were invited to attend a sumptuous lunch prior to the seminar starting. So far so good.

After lunch, everyone went into a large and comfortable sitting room with a nice fire to keep everyone warm.

The seminar host began his presentation and after thirty minutes premiered the company's glossy new video. Again, high quality all round – however, the effects of the lunch, the roaring fire and comfortable armchairs took its toll on the elderly delegates, with most of them falling asleep. To be honest, I had to pinch myself to stay awake too…

I couldn't fault the seminar itself – the venue was great and befitting of the organiser's target market. The presentation was good too – but the environment, particularly after the lunch created an extremely soporific effect that was destined to cause problems.

The message here is, choose a time for your event to suit your audience, but be mindful of external factors that could spoil things.

As to the correct day of the week, we could see in the case of the Belfast based mortgage broker that Saturdays were the best time for him.

Having said that, some days are better than others.

Try to avoid Mondays and Fridays and in order of preference, aim to go with Thursdays, Wednesdays and then Tuesdays. There is a feeling in many businesses that the serious work is done in the first half of the week (particularly Mondays).

Fridays however, can be a good day if you're running a *whole day* event and people feel that they can better justify a full day out of the office. This is particularly the case if there is a good local attraction near your event venue which they could also visit.

At the time of writing, I am planning a seminar at an hotel in Manchester, UK. The seminar is a whole day event and on a Friday. It will be finished by 4pm and the hotel is right next to Manchester United's Old Trafford stadium. As I said earlier, curiosity value is important and the fact that it is near the football ground will be sufficient to nudge some potential attendees nearer to their personal tipping point.

When running whole day events, start them after the rush hour wherever you are located. Even the most enthusiastic attendee won't want to be at your event for a full 9 to 5 day. Let them have a bit of a lie-in and go for 9.30am arrival and coffee, with a 10am start. That way everyone has a sporting chance of turning up.

Be finished by 4pm to 4.30pm so that people can either go to a local attraction or get out before the rush hour moves into full swing. If you are targeting businesspeople, avoid having an event that starts much later than 10.30am as many people will go to the office or place of work first. If they get stuck into something while they are there, then there is a good chance they will stay and miss your seminar.

But there can also be regional differences if you are thinking of putting on an event away from your usual territory. For example, timing that works well for businesspeople in Glasgow, Scotland does not necessarily work for people 70 kilometres along the M8 in Edinburgh. If you are not sure about timings at different locations, ask your venue if they have any observations on what other people do.

What about evening events?

Avoid a Friday evening unless your event has a strong social element. Good days for evening seminars are Mondays and Tuesdays. Try to make sure that evening events are held within a short walking distance of a pub or wine bar and finished by 10pm (10.30pm latest), as there is a good chance that many of your delegates will join you for a drink if you ask them. I'll explain why this happens later.

Finally, the best days to run a boot camp, retreat or residential workshop are Saturdays and Sundays and we will look at these events in more detail later.

A few further thoughts on choosing dates.

- If you are targeting businesspeople within specific trades or professions, remember to check to see if your proposed dates clash with industry events, exams or the run up to them. Not surprisingly, people taking exams will be less inclined to attend your events during this period.

- Avoid holding your events in any week which includes a public holiday. Many people take off the whole week as it reduces the amount of annual leave they need to use. I would also try to avoid the week immediately preceding one which includes a public holiday.

- Unless your product or service has specific benefits to people in the middle of summer (for example, if you manufacture ice cream), avoid holding an event between the end of June and the beginning of September.

- Do hold your events at times that benefit from seasonal activity. Financial advisers, for example, would be advised to put on some of their seminars prior to the end of the tax year.

Let's pause for a moment to recap before we move on.

- Give yourself five months or more to plan your first few seminars

- Make five decisions:

1) What are my objectives for the event? You need objectives for you, and you need an objective for your attendees (something you want them to do as a result of attending)

2) What should be the subject matter?

3) Who are my target audience and how many should attend?

4) Should I charge a fee for attendance?

5) Location, date and time

What are the five planning stages?

Broadly speaking, here's what we need to do:

- Decide what we are going to talk about and to whom
- Decide where we are going to put on our event and when
- Promote the event
- Turn up and talk
- Follow up afterwards

All this is fine, but we need a little more detail.

The five planning stages are as follows; keep to them and you won't go wrong. Here's what we're going to follow:

1. Initial preparation
2. Promotion
3. Final preparation
4. Performance
5. Post-performance

Initial Preparation

We will assume that we have already made our five decisions discussed earlier. In the initial preparation phase, we concern ourselves with the early stages of promotion together with things that should not be left to last minute (but which usually are and end up being more of a hassle than they might otherwise have been!).

Include in this phase:

- Based on your objectives for your event, work out the cost of it (even roughly) and allocate a budget. Whatever the nature of your business and type of event you are planning, you will soon see why charging for entry is such a good idea.

  Even if you decide not to charge for entry, you will discover later in this book how you can still turn your seminar or workshop into a highly profitable enterprise.

- Write a marketing plan. Once this has been done, it will form the basis of a plan to future events. Naturally as you run more events, it will be updated and improved as you learn from mistakes made earlier. The next chapter will show what should be included in your plan.

- Decide if you want to have a promotional stand or booth at your event. If you do not want to run to the expense of this, as an alternative talk to companies that make exhibition stands about branded pull-up or roller banners as these can add a very professional look to your seminar – whatever business you are in. What's more, they are really easy to store, transport and set up.

- Put together a Gantt chart to show what needs to be done and by when, or use a project management tool like Trello to keep you on track.

- If you are seeking to develop strategic partnerships with other businesses, decide if you will have other speakers present and involve them in the planning.

- Make enquiries with local business groups, colleagues or universities about possible grants or subsidies, which may be available to reduce the cost of your tickets.

- Start to build a relationship with the event or conference manager at your chosen venue (if it is not your own premises). For example, decide approximate timings for start, finish, coffee and tea breaks and agree catering ideas if appropriate.

  If you can build a relationship with the venue staff over your five-month period, believe me it will make a big difference on the day, particularly if there are any last-minute hitches.

- Write a press release and send it to your local newspapers, television and radio stations. Invite the press to attend your event and offer to write an article on your area of expertise for the paper.

  In other words, start getting your name in the media, so that when your promotion starts properly, people will recognise your name.

- Decide if you want to record or film your event and contact local video companies.

  Another option is to approach a local college or university that runs media courses, as you can often get students to help you for very low cost.

- Start to think about whether you will sell any 'back of room' products at your event. More on this in Chapter 7.

- Decide on a rough agenda for your seminar.

- Decide what equipment you will need on the day – e.g. Flipcharts, pens, screen, projector, laptop computer, overhead projector etc. Do this now so that you don't leave it to the last minute. Do not assume that the hotel or venue will have this nailed down because more often than not they don't.

  If necessary, get your own kit, particularly if you are going to do this regularly. I have my own set of flip chart pens and paper that I take with me whenever I am speaking anywhere.

- Start to spruce up your presentation skills – at the very least start thinking about some themes and ideas that you might want to present.

  Keep a notebook and write down any great words and phrases that come to mind which could be included in your presentation. There is help later in this book and there are plenty of other books and courses available.

- Start thinking about your social media activity around the event if you are promoting it publicly. Even if it is a private 'clients only' event, you might still want to tweet or post about it in advance of, during and after the event. Set up your own unique hashtag that you use right from the start.

- Put a date in the diary for your event, as this will stop you procrastinating about the whole initiative. Just do it!

Promotion

The promotion of your event is the most important aspect of all the planning. The next chapter looks at this phase in detail, but for now I will mention three important aspects which will be repeated several times.

- Make sure that all of your promotion is highly targeted. That's not to say that 'throwing enough mud in the hope that some will stick' is not a valid strategy, it's just that it takes a lot longer to get your message across to the people you want to hit. It's also the most expensive option.

- Secondly, although your promotion should be highly targeted, consider all possible methods of communication. Don't make assumptions about how people in your target market like to receive information.

- Because you won't be making assumptions about how people like to receive information, you will inevitably need to make changes to your normal marketing mix. Some changes need only be small, but they will be changes which will produce new income streams in their own right.

Final Preparation

The final preparation stage predominantly covers confirmations and rehearsals.

Included in this phase:

- Confirming advertising

- Arranging any printing that is needed

- Confirming any special equipment that needs to be hired

- Finalising your PowerPoint presentation

- Rehearsing your presentation (several times)

- If you are including case studies that involve use of software such as cashflow modelling, rehearse this multiple times so that it is clear and easy for your audience to follow

- Preparing feedback and evaluation forms

- Acknowledging bookings

- Preparing handouts

- Booking your accommodation for the night before

- Deciding what to wear on the day

- Deciding how you will follow up attendees after the event

- Arranging helpers and making sure they understand their roles

Performance

The necessary presentation skills that you will need are covered in detail later on, but there is also much else that you should consider on the day of your seminar, including:

- Avoid a heavy full English breakfast, tea or coffee. Have something light that includes fruit. Drink fruit juice or water.

- Get access to the seminar room as early as possible. It always takes longer to set up than you imagine and allow time for last minute problems.

- Even if you don't have time for a run through in the actual room, at the very least stand in the space as if the audience is present and get used to what it feels like.

- Check your technology is working (even if you checked it the night before). For example, if you are using a Windows laptop for your presentation slides, check that there isn't an update that will catch you by surprise and slow you down. If I had a pound for every time I have been caught out by this one...

- As above, if you are using cashflow modelling software (or something else) as part of your presentation, go through your examples yet again so that you are supremely confident in its use in front of an audience.

- Make sure you are completely set up before anyone arrives. You must be completely relaxed and unrushed to help ease any nerves. Once set up, try to get 20 to 30 minutes quiet time to yourself to look over your notes.

- If you do not have any secretarial support, make sure that your office phone is redirected to your mobile so that any non-attendees can get a message to you before the event starts. Ideally you will want to speak to them in person.

  Alternatively, leave a message on your office answer phone to call you on your mobile. Some people cancel by email and so you may not see their message until after the event. Attendees will also often send an email if they are going to arrive late. Setup your email to include an 'out of office' note to call you or your assistant.

- Continue to drink water (not too cold) and prepare your voice by reading out loud.

- Enjoy yourself!

Post-Performance

What you do after the event is just as important as what you do before and so you should carefully plan the post seminar activities.

These should include:

- Deciding on your immediate post event activity – i.e. while people are still there but haven't yet left the building. This is 'Golden Time' – your guests are still there, and some may be thinking about whether or not they want to come up and ask you a question.

Just because *you* have finished, doesn't mean that the event has finished for every attendee. There may be something they need an answer to that could make the difference between them becoming a customer/client or not, so don't risk blowing the opportunity to talk to people.

This is also the perfect moment to get a video testimonial or two from attendees, so this is not yet the time for you to relax.

Do you have enough resource available to handle people who want to make an appointment with you there and then – and do you have people who can take orders for any 'back of room' products that you have? More on this later.

You cannot relax until every attendee has left – and even then, I have had people return to the room unexpectedly while I'm clearing up.

- Sending out pre-prepared thank-you letters to attendees – but including your *handwritten* comments which reflect anything interesting that happened or was said on the day. Also include answers to any questions that you could not deal with at the seminar and make reference to individual comments made by people during the seminar.

- Contacting anyone who you were expecting but who did not attend.

- Analysing any feedback sheets and taking note of points raised for future events.

  A quick point on this – I'm not a big fan of feedback sheets because their completion can sometimes interrupt the flow of the event at the exact time when you want people to be motivated to come up and ask you questions personally.

  You could send feedback sheets out the following day, but then you are guaranteed that the points made will not be as enthusiastic as had they been completed on the day of your event.

  So this one is up to you as to whether or not you have any feedback sheets at all. A great alternative if you have the time, is to personally phone everyone who attended - or point people to an online feedback page on your website.

- Sending out a press release describing how the event benefited to your local attendees. If the press did not attend the event (there's never any guarantee that they will), have someone take a photo during your talk and include it with your release.

  Make sure you continue to build a relationship with the press, both locally and in the specialist press to your industry. Build on your image as an expert and this will feed through into future events which you hold. The more you contribute to the press, the more you will be perceived as an expert on your subject and the more people will want to attend your seminars.

The more people that attend your seminars, the more people will purchase your main product or service. They will also purchase other products that you have which support your seminars and we will look at this in detail in Chapter 7.

- Put in place a structured plan to contact attendees at regular intervals over the weeks and months after the event. This may include inviting them to another event in future (also see boot camps).

Summary

You can of course do too much planning for your seminars or workshops and you run the risk of getting completely bogged down in the minutiae of it all.

But I do recommend that for at least your first two or three events you try to follow some sort of plan, even if it is conceived in a pub or on the back of an envelope.

Providing you have clear objectives for what you are trying to achieve, you will find the planning stage both enjoyable and fulfilling. You will learn a great deal along the way and before long you will work out your own way of planning and promoting your events.

But our Rule of Five is a great way to start:

5 months + 5 decisions + 5 planning stages = successful seminar selling

The Golden Rules of Marketing Your Seminars

U nderstanding your business objectives and ensuring that you are visible is crucial to success.

Tony Raynor, Managing Director of Abbey Telecom, has been credited with some of the most innovative forms of marketing, including a campaign which used advertising on the side of new-born lambs.

"As a small business we cannot afford to spend huge amounts on marketing campaigns, so we have to use innovative ideas that drive people to our website or make them pick up the phone.

I met a farmer at a Round Table dinner and within the hour (and after a few glasses of wine) we agreed a sponsorship deal to provide raincoats for his new-born lambs. I knew that the bright orange raincoats would draw a lot of attention from passing motorists including several TV stations."

The campaign objective was to drive visitors to a website and included integrating the 'lamb coats' with advertising on his own engineering vehicles and works uniforms.

"I had originally thought about using Abbey Telecom and our logo but I realised that some people would be put off with a business advert so we developed a website which was an information resource for business marketers and it greatly increased our click-through to the Abbey website.

This in turn led to an increase in sales and all for a budget under £1000.

By following the campaign through we benefited from a great deal of PR in both regional and national press, increased traffic on our website and finally, and most importantly, more sales for Abbey Telecom."

Tony Raynor

In modern Seminar Selling it is not sufficient to have a room full of people to whom you make a nice presentation, in the hope that some will come up to you later with a view to purchasing your product or service. Don't get me wrong – this is a good start, but there is very much more to making your event a seriously profitable enterprise. Much more.

The marketing of your seminar or workshop is not just to promote to your event, but is integral to the presentation of you, your business, your service and your expertise. In fact, your seminar starts the moment you start marketing the event.

As I hinted at earlier in the book, to promote your events you will undoubtably have to make changes to your current marketing mix and it is the nature of these changes that will make the difference between just another seminar, and a seminar which changes your fortunes forever.

In the next chapter we will help you to make changes which will not only promote your event, but which will produce profitable new income streams in their own right.

But let's start with a few golden rules.

The most important point to remember is that your seminars are not necessarily a showcase for your main product or service. They are a showcase for your *expertise and skill,* and it is the attendees' perception of your expertise and skill which will lead to sales of your product or service.

Unless you have a substantial and specific budget to promote and run your seminar, it must at least break even and should preferably be income generating in its own right.

So to ensure that they do break even, or, to make your events as profitable as possible you need to find attendees in the most cost-effective ways possible. If you follow the rules below, you will not only promote the events, but will be well on your way to creating an exciting new income stream.

Think carefully about what I have just suggested – we're looking at a marketing activity which generates income in its own right. Now *that* is a powerful business model.

Discover what works best for you

Whatever marketing methods you adopt for your seminars, workshops and events, measure the results. It is absolutely vital to make a careful note of what *you* find to be most effective in a) getting people to attend and b) getting people to make additional purchases from you.

A marketing method that works well for me may not necessarily be the best thing for you, and just because one person finds (say) SMS messaging effective in promoting their seminar does not mean someone else will. We are all in different businesses and different parts of the world with different target clients; so when a promotional method works for you, make a detailed note of what you did and why.

But...

Don't rule out any particular method of promotion

Make sure that you try a full range of both online and traditional offline promotional methods first and do not make assumptions about how you think people want to receive information. Communication technology is changing all the time and so provides people with several different ways of sending and receiving information.

Equally, don't make assumptions about how people want to make contact with you. If for example you are a financial adviser with clients and prospects in their seventies or eighties, don't assume that they won't want to receive information by email, or on your website or by WhatsApp or Facebook Messenger.

Provide a full range of ways for people to receive your information and register for your seminar, including the tried and tested favourites:

- Email
- Via your website
- Telephone (with a freephone number)
- 24-hour telephone answering machine
- Fax (yes, some people still use fax)
- SMS/text message

- Post (postcards with either postage paid or a freepost address)
- Registration slips at the end of a mailing letter
- Face-to-face

Make your Event Irresistible!

In all your promotional activity you must strive to make your event difficult to ignore by your target audience. Do this by constantly stressing the benefits of attending your event. Benefits, benefits, benefits and then some more benefits!

Without the big marketing budgets of large corporations, small businesses have to make every communication count. And one of the best ways of doing this is to focus strongly on how, specifically, your seminar or workshop will help improve the lives of attendees – and how it has already helped others.

Offer Bonuses for Attendance

Earlier we talked about offering people discounts and incentives. Your bonuses for attendance are a key part of incentivising people.

After you have stressed the benefits, offer bonus materials for attending your event. For people who have made a decision to attend based on the advertised content, bonus materials are like the icing on the cake and help to reassure them that they have made the right decision.

For other people, what appear to be free, but high value bonuses will help to make the event irresistible so that they progress closer to their tipping point and come to the right decision.

Bonuses do two more things.

Firstly, when offered a free bonus, people feel that they are getting more than they are paying for. Something for free when they make a purchase has always been an effective draw and works particularly well in the seminar market.

Secondly, as we'll discover shortly, your seminars must in themselves offer very high content for attendees. But by offering them bonuses as well, they subconsciously believe that they will not be short-changed on content at the seminar itself.

What bonuses should I offer?

First of all, your bonuses for attendance should genuinely be of high value, and we need to prove to people that they have value.

People must believe that you really are giving them something that is not only valuable to them but to you too – like your time. Here are some examples that you could (and should) state on your promotional materials:

- Half an hour free consultation with you – valid for 12 months after the event (Value £250)

- Free question and answer email advice for 12 months after the event (Value £97)

- 25% discount on any purchase of your main product or service

- A free sample of your main product (Value £?)

- A free eBook showing attendees how to… (Value £27)

- Copy of your book (Value £12)

- Event workbook (Value £97)

- A free CD or audio recording of your event, which is only available to attendees (Value £125)

- A video copy of your seminar (Value £147)

- A weekly email after your event containing extra tips and advice (Value £97)

- 50% discount on future seminars or events that you hold (Value £47)

- Membership of your Private Facebook group (Value £125)

- Twelve months membership of your Inner Circle Mastermind Group (Value £497)

- A full refund if not completely satisfied

- Etc.

These are just a few that you could use, but think creatively how you can take your knowledge, expertise and experience and repackage it into incentives that you can give away (or sell at the back of the room or via your website) as part of the admission to your event.

You'll notice from the list above that I have noted the actual value of each item, and it's very important that you do this. Use the ideas that I have listed above, model them to your own business and highlight the value that you want to place on them.

We have all purchased products and services which have included 'freebies' at the point of sale, but this technique is much more effective when you state the value of the item(s), because this is the 'proof' that they actually have value.

As mentioned earlier, this is known as building a value stack and is particularly powerful when promoting live events such as seminars and workshops.

So you might do something like this in your promotions:

"Your investment in this unique event is £147 (discounted to £97 for immediate bookings).

And when you register today, we will put into your hands the following bonuses to say thank you for joining us:

- Free event workbook to use and take away (Value £97)
- Free video of the seminar so that you can go through it again at your leisure (Value £147)
- Free eBook *20 Easy Ways to Increase your Income in Retirement* (Value £47)

- Free 30-minute personal consultation within ten days of the event (Value £197)

- TOTAL VALUE OF BONUSES: £488"

Does that make sense?

Ideally you need the total value of your bonuses to be worth a lot more than the price of admission. In this way, you are making the price of your ticket a 'no brainer' because people won't want to miss out on all of your bonuses.

Remember, the more your bonuses are targeted at the specific needs, problems and issues of your attendees, the better - and more effective this technique will be. Another reason why targeting a niche is important when planning seminars, workshops and events.

Even if you are not charging for attendance, you should still offer bonuses and state their value. Remember, we are trying to make this event irresistible.

We will cover the importance of great copywriting later, but just a few points about the text used above.

- Note the use of "Your investment" instead of "Price". Attending your event *is* an investment – implying that it has value and that they could get a return on it.

- Note "immediate bookings". Event organisers typically use "early-bird" pricing, but in my experience, unless you are taking the best part of a year to promote your event with steadily increasing ticket prices over that period, "immediate bookings" can essentially give *anyone* the opportunity to benefit from the discount.

- Note the use of "when you register today" – planting and embedding a command in people's minds.

- Note "we will put into your hands". This is a phrase used by many top internet marketers and makes the bonuses sound more tangible and real – even if your bonuses are digital products.

- Note the repeated use of the word "free". We all love a freebie…

- Note "within ten days of the event" – creates urgency and people won't want to miss out.

Finally, when listing out your bonuses on your promotional web page or written materials, you should ideally include small images of your bonuses. So if you are giving away a CD, then you should include a picture of a CD. Even better if it is branded with your logo, photo or other image.

If you are giving away a book with your admission, then include a picture of it. You get the idea.

Get Help!

The secret behind really good promotion of a seminar is to get other people to do it for you, or to be precise – with you. Not only that, you want your promotion to be as effective as possible and for the lowest possible cost. Why make life harder for yourself when you can spread the load by asking friends and business associates for help?

Who could help?

Business Groups, Clubs and Associations

If you are the owner of a small business, there is a good chance that you are a member of a national or local business club or association.

It could be the local Rotary, Chamber of Commerce, export club, networking group etc., and this means you have access to dozens, if not hundreds or even thousands of other business people, many of whom may want your product or service (or even to attend your event).

That's great, but even better is that these clubs and associations are always looking for new members, so offer them a free advertisement in your seminar handout, leaflet or workbook. In exchange they may be prepared to include your event in their club magazine, paper or email newsletter.

This idea also extends to local sports and special interest clubs. They are also looking for new members, so approach them in the same way.

In addition to being included in their newsletters, they might even do something really old-school like put your promotional leaflet on their club noticeboard – or at the other end of the scale post tweets about how excited they are to be sponsoring your event.

You may even be able to get local business and sports clubs to sponsor your event, providing you with either cash, promotional reach or both. They will want their logo on your promotional materials and website, but this will add extra credibility to your seminar.

In short, use the power and reach of local organisations to help promote your event.

Newspapers and Magazines

Just like business groups above, there is great potential to obtain free publicity from newspapers and magazines.

A journalist friend once told me to create news out of everything your business does and to tell your local and industry press accordingly. Do the same with your seminar – however small your business is. If it's newsworthy, has a great hook and tells a good story it will more often than not get printed.

Send a press release to your local newspaper about your seminar or workshop, explaining what your event is about and how people will benefit.

Read the news articles on the first two or three pages of your local newspaper to get a feel for their style; then try to write your release in the same way so that a busy editor need only directly copy what you have written.

Remember to send a professionally taken photograph and include a quote from yourself, which can also be copied directly, e.g.:

"Proprietor of Collins Jams & Preserves, Susan Collins commented today: 'We're really excited about our new open day in November.

We've had so many customers ask us over the years about our recipes and how we make our jams, so this will be a superb opportunity for people to see the process in action. What's more, there will be free samples to take away!"

Yes, an 'open day' is a great live marketing opportunity too.

Always follow up your press release with a telephone call. Don't hassle the editor or ask them if they are going to print something, but enquire politely if they received the release and whether they have all the information they need.

You can also offer to write an article about your area of expertise and explain how this would benefit both the paper and its readers. Remember – benefits, benefits, benefits.

Only this week I asked a leading blogger if he would be able to promote an event that I am running, and he agreed on the basis that I would write a one-thousand-word article for his website.

Finally, some local papers will be very happy to 'sponsor' your event by putting their name to it.

Offer to present your seminar 'in association with the *County Times*' for example, in exchange for them giving you a free advertisement or for publishing an article about your business.

Explain that you are happy to publicise the paper in all your promotional materials and the seminar handouts without charge if they are able to help you in this way. Although the newspaper will have little, if any involvement in the event, the lending of their name will enhance the credibility of your seminar.

Equally, if there is a specialist magazine serving your industry you can try the same approach, only do it earlier as magazine content is decided much further in advance. The newspaper or magazine concerned may even be prepared to give you free copies to give out to your attendees, again enhancing the value of the event.

Radio Stations

Here in the UK access to a good choice of speech-based radio stations is improving all the time, with BBC local radio offering an excellent service.

We also have a wide range of digital stations with whom we could build relationships if we play our cards right, in much the same way as newspapers above.

There are many commercial stations too, but these generally have far less speech-based material. Either way, make the effort to build a relationship with your local stations.

Local commercial radio works hard at not just entertaining, but at adding value and is often open to suggestions for new slots as long as it fits with their format. You may be able to suggest a new slot which will not only hold you up as the local expert, but which should also get you a great deal of free publicity. Even if you can't get a regular slot, if you have taken the trouble to build a relationship and are seen as friendly and personable, there is a good chance that you could be featured on a 'phone in' or even interviewed.

I know of several financial advisers who have regular radio slots, and without exception they have all found them valuable.

Podcasts

In much the same way that we can build relationships with local radio stations, we can also do the same thing with podcasts and their hosts.

When I first wrote this book in 2003, there were no podcasts – certainly not as we know them today.

But in essence, *anyone* can now set up their own radio station from the comfort of their own home or office, and there are countless podcasts which have the potential to feature you, your business and your seminars, events and workshops.

Many podcasts are run on the interview format where the host interviews guests from all walks of life and business. If you have expertise in a given area or specialism, it's entirely reasonable to hope that you could be interviewed on someone's podcast.

I've been interviewed multiple times for podcasts around the world, giving me a platform to both add value and, when appropriate, promote by products and services.

There's a kind of unwritten rule that if you are invited onto a podcast, you are given the opportunity to promote yourself, your website or whatever.

Whilst this gives us the tantalising opportunity to promote our events far and wide (which is a good thing), you still want to try and focus on attracting attendees to your seminar who are local – or at least within striking distance.

There are multiple podcast directories out there, so I'm not going to list any here, but just Google 'podcast directories' and you'll find the latest and most up to date. But given that you ideally want local attendees for your event, a good thing to do is to go into Facebook groups that are local to you and ask people if they know of any podcast hosts who are local.

When you have a list, approach the hosts in much the same way as approaching a local newspaper, club or organisation. I would suggest spending time building the relationship before you tell them that what you are really after is an opportunity to promote your event. It's a bit like connecting with people on LinkedIn – build a dialogue long before you start trying to sell anything.

Quite apart from promotion of your event, building relationships with podcast hosts can also have profound and valuable benefits for your business in the medium and longer term.

And again, if a podcast host agrees to mention your seminar or event, also offer to highlight their podcast in your seminar handouts etc.

Later on we will look at the benefits of financial advisers having their own podcast.

Instagram, YouTubers and Influencers

Just like a podcast, any of us can now have our very own TV channel – on YouTube or Vimeo, another high-quality video platform.

Some Instagrammers and YouTube channel hosts (also known as influencers) have huge followings, and with careful outreach to them, you may well be able to strike up a relationship, which in time could lead to them promoting your event.

As before, it's about the value that you can add to them so that they can grow their channel – whether that's an appearance on one of their videos or Instagram stories, or promoting their channel in your seminar materials – or both.

Why is approaching influencers important to consider as part of your promotional plan? Take a look at these stats from Sujan Patel at bigcommerce.co.uk:

- When it comes to millennials, only 1% of them trust advertisements. However, 33% of them trust blog reviews for their purchases

- Around 40% of people reported that they purchased a product online after seeing it used by an influencer on YouTube, Instagram, or Twitter

- 71% of influencers believe that it's an honest and authentic voice that keeps their audience engaged

- 48% of marketers say they plan to ramp up their budget for influencer-focused campaigns

- According to a study by Tomoson, influencer marketing yields a $6.50 return on investment for every dollar spent.

As Anand Kansal at Outgrow highlights:

"The great thing about influencer marketing is that you can kill three birds with one stone – create great content, earn credibility and gain exposure through the influencer's network."

Influencer marketing has always been powerful, but since the advent of social media – particularly YouTube and Instagram, it has grown rapidly in popularity.

We could write a whole book on the topic, but a Google search for 'Influencer outreach' will give you much more information. My job is to highlight that it can be used as an additional way to promote your seminars and events.

And don't forget local influencers – there will almost always be high profile individuals in your local community who can provide promotional assistance either online or through their own communication channels.

Friends, Staff and Colleagues

In much the same way as in all of the above, offer real incentives for friends and colleagues to promote your seminar. The number of people you can potentially reach is multiplied many times over if you have several people helping you. But as mentioned earlier, you must make it worth their while.

People in Similar Businesses

Don't shy away from approaching people in a similar business or marketplace to yourself. Remember, the object of the exercise is to get bums on seats and ideally, targeted bums on seats. Where better than the customers and clients of similar businesses?

Approach these businesses directly and offer a 50% share of any paid registrations obtained as a result of registrations coming via them. Yes, be that generous in order to get their attention.

Businesses will often cooperate and collaborate with others when they can see mutual benefits. They won't go as far as letting you contact their clients but will often partner with a similar business in certain markets where there is potential for a win-win situation.

There is no earthly reason why two or more financial advice businesses shouldn't team up to host a joint event aimed at their local community.

Bring a Friend

A great way to dramatically increase attendance is to tell people that they can bring a friend or colleague. Very often this approach can double the number of your attendees. And if you are charging for attendance you can either offer the friend's ticket at half price, or even free. It works – try it!

'Dream 100'

This is a longer-term strategy, but one which is hugely powerful when you commit to it.

ClickFunnels founder Russell Brunson talks about The Dream 100 which has been at the heart of how he gets influential clients and connections to promote his software services. It's a simple concept but makes a lot of sense.

Russell discovered the Dream 100 concept from the late Chet Holmes in his book *The Ultimate Sales Machine* and adapted it for the modern marketing environment.

In essence you need to find one hundred clients, connections or high-profile individuals who could potentially promote your products or services – or in this case your events.

You then need to build strong relationships with them, so that in time, they feel that it is the most natural thing in the world to support you as a partner.

To get to this point, you will need to:

- Regularly provide them with value – in the early days as often as monthly

- Send them educational information of relevance

- Promote their own products and services

- Be creative and send personalised videos and video emails

- Subscribe to their blogs and social media channels

- Tag or mention them in your own social media posts and content

- Purchase their products and services

- Attend their own events

- Feature them and their products/services in your own blogs, videos, podcasts etc.

In short, help them to regularly hear your name by being a strong advocate for them.

Where can you find these people?

- Amongst your clients
- Professional or other business introducers with whom you already have a relationship
- Local, high profile businesspeople
- List owners
- Bloggers, vloggers and online influencers
- Podcasters
- Social Media

Your current client list is a great place to start, because the chances are that you already have some 'raving fans' and keen advocates among them. These people will be far easier to approach, with some of them being extremely eager to help you.

Even if you can't come up with a hundred people, you should be able to find ten to twenty, and this is plenty to get you going.

As I said at the start of this section, this is a longer-term strategy because you first need to further strengthen already good relationships, so it's worth spending time brainstorming a plan of attack in a way that adds value but without appearing creepy or spammy.

Think carefully about each name on your list and figure out what they would find of value in their own lives or business. For example, if they have a blog, there's a fair chance that they would like even more subscribers, so think about how you could publicise it for them.

Over time – usually the course of six months to a year, it will become apparent that you are a loyal advocate for them and in time they will feel more than inclined to want to support your own initiatives – in this case your seminars and events.

Affiliates

By now you should be able to see a number of cost-effective ways to get a room full of attendees for your event, whether a small gathering in your shop or office premises or something a little larger in a hotel or other venue.

Yes, a carefully thought-through marketing plan will be important, but a key part of it should always be to get as much help as possible from other people and businesses.

As in the last section, these people will often be more than happy to help you if you have in turn supported them. But it's worth mentioning the obvious here – consider paying them as well.

In short, if you are charging for attendance, consider offering a generous commission for introductions that go on to purchase a ticket. Fifty percent is pretty generous, and you will often find that people will help you on this basis.

There are a number of ways to identify who has introduced paying attendees to you, through some ready-made online affiliate tools that plug into your website. Or, introducers could be given a unique identifier code that they ask paying delegates to use when signing up.

Some website software packages also offer tools that you can use to track introductions and pay affiliate commissions, such as the Backpack facility within ClickFunnels - ClickFunnels being a powerful tool to help you easily create landing pages for your event and other business projects requiring an online presence.

If you have not heard of ClickFunnels, you can get a free trial via the link on my website at www.philipcalvert.com/resources

Involve your Community

As we have seen, hosting a seminar, workshop or event is a powerful and proven way to promote your financial advice business and to attract new clients. There are also several other reasons why you might host such an event – perhaps to raise your profile locally, create a new income stream or build relationships with people who can introduce new clients.

But another, often overlooked approach is to involve your wider community in your events.

A great example of this is schools – particularly smaller schools in rural environments who struggle to raise funds for maintenance, building repairs or even larger projects such as purchasing and installing a piece of equipment or laying a synthetic football pitch.

Traditionally schools have relied on the generosity of parents through donations - plus hosting of quiz nights, cake and jumble sales and other activities. Whilst these can work well, it is often very hard work and only happens at all thanks to a considerable amount of time and effort put in by teachers, parents and carers.

But an approach which has proven to be effective is to broaden the school's life and activities to become an integral part of the wider local community.

A great place to start is to get far more involved with social media – particularly local Facebook groups and Twitter where many community activities and initiatives tend to congregate.

Other things schools can do to embed themselves further into the local community include:

- Open the school up to non-school events
- Host music showcases
- Host local debates
- Host civic events
- Host sports events

- Host walks that begin and end at the school
- Host arts and craft events
- Create a community garden

Schools should also set out to interact, engage with and support organisations such as Brownies and Boy Scouts, plus local business organisations like Rotary and Chamber of Commerce. By building partnerships with these groups, you will help to cement your school's cultural role in the community.

Where schools have worked hard to build relationships within the local community, it has often resulted in substantial investments being made in support of their projects. And it can often be as simple as resulting in a local company providing paint and materials to redecorate classrooms. Some companies will even provide staff at weekends to come along and do the work for you.

It's not always small local companies that will provide support if given the opportunity to engage with your school. Metro Bank has been known to get involved as have others such as DIY store B&Q. But it won't happen unless you have a strategy of reaching out and opening your school to the local community.

Now think about your own business, and brainstorm ways that you could broaden the scope of your seminars and events to encompass the wider community – or indeed aspects of it where you feel you can add value.

As a firm of financial advisers, with careful thought, there could be multiple ways that you could interact, engage and embed yourself in your local community.

In so doing you will raise your profile significantly, which in turn will ultimately produce the commercial results that you are seeking.

Offline and Online Marketing and Promotion

"Businesses don't want radio commercials; they want advertising that works. The biggest mistake radio advertisers make is that they think creativity will generate a higher response rate. This is not true.

Creativity 'in itself' won't persuade anyone to buy a product or service. It is there to lead the listener's mind in the direction we want it to go.

This sounds contradictory, but no matter how bizarre the scenario in your radio ad – always keep it real. If the listener can't connect with the scenario, they will not know what to do and why they should do it."

Alan Bell, former Chief Executive, Airforce

In the previous chapter we started to examine some of the rules of marketing your seminars. To recap, the really important points to remember are:

- Initially, unless you know your target market extremely well, do not rule out any particular type of promotional method.

- Do not make assumptions about how people want to receive information.

- Do not make assumptions about how people will want to register for your seminar. Provide a full range of options.

- Make your event irresistible to your target market, so they just *have* to attend.

- Provide a number of financial incentives to attend, such as discounts for early booking, discounts for bulk bookings, discounts for members of business clubs and groups.

- Offer worthwhile bonuses for attendance and state their value as a package.

- Encourage people who want to attend to bring a friend – either free or at a substantial discount.

- Work closely with business clubs, friends, colleagues, associates and other businesses to promote your events. Consider offering strong monetary incentives for each person they introduce and who registers to attend.

- Work with the local press to raise your company's profile by writing articles for their publication. Also, build relationships with local radio stations.

- Provide publicity for local business groups and media by offering them free advertising on your seminar promotional materials and handouts.

- Expand the benefits of your events into the wider community.

- Measure the effectiveness of everything you do. Take careful note of what works and what doesn't for next time.

- Whatever you do, constantly stress the benefits of your event. Remember – benefits, benefits and more benefits!

Everything that you do here, helps people to reach their personal tipping point where they feel that it is the most natural thing to commit to attending.

In short, work with as many people as possible to get your message out there, because this is key to successful promotion of your event. It can be extremely hard work to do it all on your own and unless you have a large advertising budget you need as many people as possible helping you.

Essentially you have two main ways of promoting your events:

1. Offline promotion
2. Online promotion

OFFLINE PROMOTION

Until the arrival of the internet, promotion of seminars was restricted to traditional offline activities. Predominantly these were, and still are:

- Advertising in newspapers and magazines (both local and national)
- Articles in local papers and magazines
- Articles in industry publications and press

- Promotions at local community events
- Promotions and networking through Chamber of Commerce
- Direct mail
- Leaflet drops
- Handouts at trade shows
- Posters
- Postcards
- Telephone
- Television and Radio advertising
- Audio and video in CD or DVD format
- Business introducers, word of mouth and advocates
- Joint ventures and collaborations
- Public relations (PR)
- SMS messaging
- General correspondence
- Fax marketing!

Let's have a look at some of these promotional methods in more detail, because they all still have a valuable part to play.

Television and Radio Advertising

Television advertising is likely to be well out of reach of most small businesses until digital television becomes even more commonplace, but it is worth talking about the benefits of radio advertising in more detail.

Radio advertising for the promotion of your seminar can be extremely effective at a local level. It's not as expensive as you might think and there are a variety of packages available.

Consider the facts:

According to research undertaken by the Radio Advertising Bureau, around two-thirds of the adult population tune in to radio each week and over 80% each month. There is a fairly even split in listening by gender, with 67% of men and 65% of women listening each week.

The favourite places for listening are generally those where radio accompanies another activity – e.g. in the car, over breakfast, in the bathroom, at the gym and at the workplace. Radio often accompanies other media such as reading newspapers and magazines, surfing the internet and even watching television!

Around 65% of all adults listen to the radio in-car every week. Approximately 73% of in-car listeners fall into the ABC1 socio-economic group with 56% falling in to the C2DE group.

The highest percentage of in-car listeners fall into the 25 to 44 age group, falling slightly for those aged 45 and above. The in-car audience has a strong skew towards upmarket, young to middle age men – an important audience who tend to be light commercial television viewers.

The good news is that over two-thirds of businesspeople listen to commercial radio, and on average they will listen for over 12 hours a week – longer than they spend watching television.

This is much higher than is usually assumed – in fact businesspeople spend more time each day listening to radio than any other key media (such as television, newspapers and magazines).

The Importance of Radio

Reflecting perhaps today's more relaxed working environment in modern Britain, radio listening at work has increased noticeably in recent years.

For advertisers who are targeting a business audience, the key issue is effective 'cut-through'. Conventional business media are very cluttered, and businesspeople have learned to edit ruthlessly – especially with printed media.

And despite the fact that radio stations broadcast to millions of people, they are still talking to one person at a time. This is particularly significant to the businessperson alone in their car, because approximately 70% of commercial station listeners do not change channels when the advertisements are on. This differs from television viewers, where a similar percentage admit to flicking through the other channels or fast-forwarding when the advertisements start.

There is evidence to show that people feel a sense of trust in their radio station – very valuable in an age where television and newspapers are not as trusted as they used to be and there is good evidence to suggest that people actively listen to the radio even though they might be doing something else.

One of the most important points about radio though is that it is becoming more widely available thanks to technology. For example, radio via a mobile phone is rapidly increasing in popularity due to the incredible rise of podcasts – particularly through apps such as BBC Sounds.

In conclusion, in tandem with the inexorable rise of the internet, radio is extremely important in the lives of its listeners and, combined with other media (which is often consumed simultaneously), radio can be extraordinarily effective. Quite apart from using the medium to promote your main business, it should definitely be considered as a way of promoting your seminars.

If you don't have budget for radio advertising, consider building relationships with local radio journalists and aim to be featured on phone-in programmes.

And when combined with other forms of local promotion, the effect can be impressive.

For example…

Sponsoring Roundabouts

Now we're stepping into more old school territory. In fact, territory is the name of the game here.

When it comes to sponsoring a roundabout, you have two options:

Firstly, it can be as simple as having a sign on a busy roundabout that says 'Sponsored by Jones & Co Independent Financial Advisers' – possibly including your phone number or website address.

Or secondly, you have a sponsorship arrangement where you work with the local council concerned to assist with the roundabout's maintenance and care – but with the focus on the environmental aspect by making it look attractive, plant flowers, trees etc. and attract wildlife. Whilst this is great news for the local area, it is of course valuable PR which will bear fruit over time.

What are the advantages of sponsoring a roundabout in your area?

- You differentiate yourself from your competitors

- Very high footfall or eyeballs on your advertising board

- Many people will see your advertisement several times a day – repeated exposure is important for success with advertising

- You become the only advertiser in that location, whereas local newspapers may carry multiple advertisements for competitors

- Unlike TV or radio advertising, your advertisement can't be muted or turned over – it's difficult to ignore!

- Newspaper advertising typically has a shelf life of one day – most roundabout opportunities are 24/7 for up to twelve months

- Newspaper audiences are falling, whilst traffic levels are increasing

So if you are a local business that wants to raise awareness and send people to your website where they will see your seminar promotion, then roundabout advertising or sponsorship could be a great idea for you, particularly when combined with other forms of local promotion.

It certainly was for Keith Churchouse of Chapters Financial in Guildford who combined roundabout advertising with local radio appearances and said:

"We sponsored roundabouts for many years, which made a huge difference. Clients would hear me on the radio, see the name on a roundabout, then get in touch."

Telephone

The telephone should certainly be considered as part of your armoury when marketing to existing clients. A relationship already exists for starters. Expect around half to say they are interested in your seminar and half of these to actually turn up.

Clearly, we need to be mindful of the fact that cold calling is not permitted if people have not given you permission to call. Quite apart from anything else, cold calling has reached epidemic proportions and is usually unwanted by recipients.

I would also go so far as to say that you should avoid calling even existing clients with the sole purpose of promoting your seminars and events. Such conversations should be restricted to being included as part of other business conversations that you were having anyway on the telephone.

Either way, use this approach with caution and aim to be professional and courteous at all times, because the last thing you want is to gain a reputation for being a telephone spammer.

Direct Mail

There are two types of direct mailshot: addressed mail and unaddressed mail.

Addressed mail

As I was putting out the dustbin for collection this morning, our postman Jim was just arriving. He reached inside his bag and said, *"Shall I put these in the bin here and now to save you the trouble of taking them in the house?"*

Not surprisingly, Jim's perception of the effectiveness of direct mail is a little prejudiced, but nevertheless it does have significant benefits.

Perhaps the main benefit of addressed direct mail is the ability to precisely target specific types of customer or potential customer. Combined with an infinite range of creative possibilities, direct mail has much more going for it than you might imagine, though it's tempting to think that in our electronic age mail would be losing its appeal.

But when *combined* with a variety of other media it continues to offer enormous possibilities. And unlike email marketing, direct mail gives you greater freedom to reach out, connect and sell – though you are always advised to ensure that your mail recipients have a genuine and legitimate interest in receiving it.

According to the Data & Marketing Association (DMA), the art of mail marketing is far from dead. Sending marketing material by post is on the rise, with the DMA reporting a 43% increase in customer responses to direct mail.

What's more, the DMA reports that on average, people keep their post for 38 days. To put this in perspective, 51% of emails are deleted within two seconds.

Again, quoting the DMA:

"In case you don't already know, legitimate interest is a term coined by the Information Commissioner's Office (ICO) that offers greater flexibility for customer data processing.

Businesses that send direct mail can do so on the basis of legitimate interest. They do not need to record consent from the recipient.

What you do need to ensure is this:

- *That the use of data is valid*
- *Direct mail has a minimal impact on privacy*
- *Is expected by the recipient or they won't be surprised to receive it*

Let's say a customer purchases a product from you online - does that signal legitimate interest in your business?

Absolutely. They have actively engaged with your products and wouldn't be shocked to see your catalogue or brochure on their doorstep. Additionally, if a customer has previously opted-in to your marketing emails, you can send them direct mail on the basis that they've proven their interest."

Either way, let's use some common sense here and save ourselves some money at the same time. There is very little point in sending out mailing letters that are not relevant to their recipient, so good targeting is essential – and the people most likely to respond favourably to your direct mailings are your existing clients and people with whom you have commercial relationships. And even then, you should choose your recipients with care.

The effectiveness of your mailing campaign can be improved further if you think carefully about the content and copywriting in your mailing. Always keep in mind who your target market is and adapt your message and language accordingly.

Some things you might want to consider:

- Addressed mail means just that – use their name and spell it correctly

- Consider hand-writing the *"Dear Sue"* or *"Dear John"* salutation

- Have a powerful headline or title to your letter. It should ideally be in the form of a question, implying that you have the answer if they take action

A strong title is vital, so make it count. Remember, benefits, benefits and more benefits. For example:

"Are you looking for easy ways to increase the value of your home?"

"Have you ever wondered how to value antiques like the experts?"

"Are you looking for easy ways to improve fitness without paying for expensive gym membership?"

Play around with this format and adapt it for your own event.

Other points to note in your mailing:

- Consider putting your headline or title in "quotation marks". This gives the impression that someone actually said it so there is a human touch behind it.

- Should the mailing be sent by first or second-class post?

  First class is better, because the recipient of a second-class letter subconsciously feels that they are not considered very important

- Would a handwritten envelope make a difference?

  Again, put yourself in the shoes of the recipient. If it's handwritten it might be from a relative or friend and is far more likely to be opened. It also feels personalised to the recipient and people often associate good news with handwritten envelopes (birthday cards with cheques inside!)

- Add additional personalisation touches.

  For example, attach a brightly coloured Post-It or sticky note to the letter with a short handwritten message along the lines of *"Would love to have you join us Mike. This is perfect for you…"*.

Marketers often report take-up rates increasing dramatically with touches like this. There is also evidence to show that even attaching a blank sticky note can increase take up!

- What typeface should be used?

   Wherever possible use a font which is professional, yet easy to read, like Times New Roman or other 'Serif' fonts like Palatino or Bookman Old Style. 'Sans-serif' fonts went through a period of being popular, but tastes are reverting back to Serif because they appear to give your text a little more gravitas.

- Would the quality of the envelope and paper make a difference?

   This depends on your market, but my view is always opt for the best possible quality within the context of your target audience.

- What is the best day for people to receive your mailing?

   I am not convinced that it makes much difference what day of the week your mailing arrives, though there are schools of thought that suggest you should avoid mail arriving on a Monday. It's true that Monday's mail often seems to have less important stuff in it, so perhaps you don't want to give the impression that yours is not important too.

- Arrange the material in the envelope so that when opened, the first thing people see is their name.

  Using the recipient's name makes the piece look more personal and should increase the chances of it being read.

- Within the body of your letter use 'trial closes'. You do this by making a point or highlight a success story and then say something like, *"Does that make sense?"* or *"Does that sound good?"* This subconsciously gets people saying 'yes' and helps to nudge people to their tipping point.

- Always include a 'PS' at the end of your letter and make sure it includes one of the most important benefits of attending your seminar. The 'PS' is virtually always read, so it must contain a key benefit of attending.

  One trick that some marketers use is to summarise the whole letter in the PS saying something like, *"If you're like me and often skip to the end, here's what you won't want to miss out on…"* etc.

The Personal Profile

An often-overlooked aspect of your direct mailing (and indeed online marketing) is the personal profile.

All too often, seminar marketers either forget or don't realise the importance highlighting information about the speaker(s) or presenter(s) at their events.

Quite apart from the content that is being presented, potential attendees will also be drawn to the individuals involved – even if they have never heard of you before. Humans are hardwired to be interested in other people's story – how they came to be who they are, what shaped them as people etc., so your marketing materials should include this information.

Don't skimp on detail either.

Earlier I mentioned Nido Qubein, who includes a two-page information sheet in his promotional materials about who he is, how he got to where he is today and why he is the person to be hosting the event.

Nido also includes two photos of himself on the information sheet – one of him looking fairly formal (a bit like a LinkedIn profile photo) and the other in a more relaxed situation – giving readers an opportunity to feel as though they have got to know him.

Whatever you do with your event mailing materials, always put yourself in the shoes of the recipient and do whatever it takes to get the piece opened and read.

But the key factors are always going to be personal, precise targeting of your offering with information on specifically how your seminar will be of benefit and how it has benefited others before them.

Unaddressed Mail

Although the ability to target clients using addressed mail is much more effective, unaddressed mail is still very popular. And don't we know it! Everything from brochures, leaflets, magazines, free samples and money-off vouchers are delivered to houses and businesses across the country every day.

Only this morning, my post included six unaddressed pieces, one of which I even pinned up on our kitchen noticeboard. Can you guess what it was?

Yes, it was an updated version of our local Chinese takeaway's menu.

But despite the apparent overload of direct mail, it can be extremely effective. Once it has dropped through your letterbox you have to do something with it and for a brief moment you are forced to look at it.

And if it's been carefully targeted there's a good chance you'll hold onto it for a little bit longer. In fact, some types of unaddressed direct mail are deliberately retained – particularly catalogues and items that contain helpful information.

I'm a firm believer that mailings of any description need to be particularly carefully targeted to be effective, but when promoting your seminars there can definitely be a place for unaddressed mail.

A supply of well-produced leaflets can be sent to a variety of different clubs and business groups for distribution to members and you can also arrange for leaflets to be inserted into copies of local newspapers or magazines. Friends and colleagues can distribute your leaflets too, and also consider including one with every piece of regular mail that leaves your office or business premises.

In addition, you can also do a local leaflet drop where you can put one through the letterbox of every house or business in a certain area. Obviously, the more targeted you can make your leaflet drop, the better.

The best types of unaddressed direct mail are those that are useful – menus, club opening times, local discount vouchers etc. Take a moment to think how you could create a leaflet that recipients actually want to keep.

Press Advertising

First, paid press advertising.

Traditional press advertising is, not surprisingly, the first port of call for many seminar hosts. You have the advantage of knowing that your advertisement is going to be seen by thousands, if not hundreds of thousands of people either in your local vicinity or wider still.

The general rule of thumb is that the more you advertise, the more your information will be seen and theoretically the greater likelihood of a response. It follows that the greater you want the response to be, the more you will have to pay. But it doesn't always have to be that way.

Certainly, creativity has a part to play in the effectiveness of your advertisement, as does clarity, perception of expertise, perception of value, targeting and the degree to which the benefits of attending are explained.

It is also extremely important to have some sort of properly organised advertising plan or campaign, rather than rely on just one big advertisement a week or two before your event.

Businesspeople who successfully use seminars as part of their overall marketing strategy will usually have developed their own advertising plans which they have put together through trial and error over time.

Positioning and frequency of your advertisements is also extremely important.

Here's what independent financial adviser and regular seminar host, Andrew Brown told me:

"We have always adopted a very direct approach [to advertising our seminars] and we found that to maximise the response to the event you would need a run of advertisements in the local press (in a prominent place in the paper – an 'early right' being ideal) over a four week period.

A single advert would never be sufficient, and the responses would tend to be greatest for the second week, with a considerable overflow into the third and final week prior to the event.

The last advertisement should be at least a week beforehand and it was always beneficial to top up the numbers with invitations to both existing and potential professional introducers with a number of carefully selected clients."

The best thing to do is to talk to the advertising executives at your local paper and enquire as to packages that they can offer you.

Free Press Advertising

There is nothing like getting free advertising when it comes to promoting your seminars! Advertising can take up a sizeable chunk of your budget, so anything you can get free will help.

As we mentioned earlier, send regular press releases to your local paper and offer to write a series of articles. The editors will often pick up on a good press release and write an editorial. Sometimes it will just be a few lines and on other occasions something more substantial. Later on, we will look at how to find material for your release.

Also as mentioned earlier, try to come to some sort of reciprocal arrangement where you promote your event in association with the paper.

SMS Messaging

SMS/text marketing has been described as a hidden gem amongst the marketing world yet is still seen as a relatively new marketing communication tool amongst small businesses - despite the first text message in the UK being sent in December 1992 (source: text.it).

It has done rather well since then with approximately 23 billion being sent each day worldwide.

According to techjury:

- While not everyone has a smartphone with internet access, 5 billion people in the world can send and receive SMS messages.

- 75% of consumers are OK with receiving SMS messages from brands (after they've opted in).

- SMS messages have a whopping 98% open rate.

- Text messages have a 209% higher response rate than phone, email, or Facebook.

- 90% of SMS messages are read within 3 minutes.

- Consumers redeem SMS-delivered coupons 10 times more than other types of coupons.

So as a marketer, what's not to like?!

Many of us have subscribed to receive regular service texts, e.g.:

- Texts from the bank to advise us on our account balance
- Information on football scores
- Betting tips
- News updates
- Weather reports
- Traffic reports
- Horoscopes
- Help to quit smoking
- Etc.

And according to one survey, 14% of mobile users have even used text messaging to end a relationship!

Here are some other ways that it is used:

- To send short, instant communication such as reminders and instructions to groups of people.

- To convey the same message to groups of people for the same price as sending it to one person.

- To receive advertisements jobs and vacancies – either from within an organisation or a recruitment company.

- To communicate with staff in the field or overseas in a cost-effective manner.

- To enhance the perception of your customer service.

- To use in a sales situation by targeting business messages at specific groups of people.

- To announce special offers and bargains.

- To announce seminars and workshops.

- To enable people to register their place at a seminar.

- To issue digital, money-off vouchers.

- To announce competitions.

- To build and enhance your brand.

Clearly many organisations also do much of the above through mobile apps using the internet, but SMS is still very popular and can be a useful and different addition to your communications mix.

As a tool for the seminar organiser, SMS technology clearly has much to offer and is invaluable for not only promoting an event, but in helping to remind people who have booked to actually turn up! So for example, when people register for your event, encourage them to opt into text reminders.

I often use text messaging to follow up a presentation. This has to be done on the same day as your talk to be effective and involves sending a text to all the attendees who have opted in and goes along the lines of:

"I hope you enjoyed our talk today – thank you for all the kind comments afterwards. If you have any additional questions, please reply to this message, call or email and I'll be happy to help. Meanwhile, you can find additional information and resources - and news of a special offer exclusive to today's attendees at www.philipcalvert.com. Thanks again and great to meet you today! Philip Calvert"

Often, as many as 70% of the attendees will send a quick reply.

Just make sure that you put something on your website for them to see! I have also used texting to follow up people who have attended my stand at exhibitions and conferences, and I have often had people come back to find me proudly showing my text on their phone!

When sending 'post event' texts, send them about 90 to 180 minutes after it finishes. Texts in business unbelievably still have novelty value and the recipient will often be surprised to hear from you in this way.

Just remember, make sure that people have opted in to receive your texts. Make a habit of explaining to new clients and customers when you first meet them, that you occasionally send out useful communications by text and that to receive them, they need to opt in. Most people will be more than happy to register provided that they can be reassured that you won't spam them and that they will only receive texts of genuine value.

Public Relations (PR)

We have mentioned the importance of using a press release to try and obtain free publicity for your business and your seminars.

Whilst one-off releases can be effective, they are more so as part of a planned and structured campaign where you have made the effort to build a relationship with the press over time.

Outright promotion of your business in the form of a press release is not necessarily going to get you the publicity you are looking for; there needs to be something newsworthy about what you are doing and generally that means offering something that is seen to be different, entertaining or significant. But of course, where your events are part of a wider community initiative, you are much more likely to get coverage.

This is another reason why I recommend you take a full five months to plan and put together your events; to give yourself time to build a relationship with the press. You can do this yourself, but there are numerous PR firms who can assist with this important part of your promotion.

At the heart of good PR is the ability to communicate the good reputation of a business or individual and this sits very nicely with one of the key objectives behind seminar marketing – to enhance the perception of your expertise.

In the meantime, get into the habit of telling the press about everything you do – however trivial you might think it is.

- If you have won an important new contract for your business – tell the press.

- If you have sent your staff on a customer service course – tell the press.

- If you have sponsored the local bowls club – tell the press.

- If you and some colleagues are running in the London Marathon – tell the press.

- If you are hosting a local seminar or event – tell the press.

You get the idea…

And when you do send out a press release, also add it to the News section of your website. Financial Life Planners Serenity Financial Planning posted a copy of their press release after they had hosted a client event at Lincoln Cathedral.

Here's what they said:

Press Release

For Immediate Release

- Local independent financial planner hosts exclusive client event
- Clive Thompson of Serenity Financial Planning hosts first exclusive client event at the Cathedral Centre, Lincoln
- Exciting news and developments within Serenity Financial Planning announced over Canapés and Prosecco
- Clive Thompson showcased how a new approach to financial planning is proving popular in Lincoln

26 September 2016 – Clive Thompson of Serenity Financial Planning, Lincoln, hosted an exclusive evening called *'Canapés by Lincoln Cathedral'* with his clients at The Cathedral Centre, Minster Yard, Lincoln on Thursday 22nd September.

Clive provided an update on some exciting developments within Serenity Financial Planning including becoming a Registered Life Planner through the Kinder Institute of Life Planning.

Clive explained how Financial Life Planning takes traditional financial planning to another level by focussing on our more deeply held values, beliefs and aspirations that influence what we do. Those plans and dreams we've put off that were they to be included in a financial plan would lead to a more fulfilling life.

Clive went on to explain why he had pursued becoming a Financial Life Planner describing his journey from a traditional product-focused financial adviser to one that forges long term relationships with his clients focussing on their whole life and not just their money.

Serenity Financial Planning is the largest Financial Life Planning firm in the UK coupling coaching with truly independent financial planning to help clients really figure out what they want out of life before helping them realise their dreams and aspirations.

Clive commented,

"This event was everything I'd hoped it would be and more. Not only were my clients able to learn more about Financial Life Planning and our business, they were able to meet several members of the Serenity Team for the first time including founder Tina Weeks. All in a beautiful location.

The feedback has been amazing and it's inspired me to make this an annual event"

Tina Weeks of Serenity Financial Planning said,

"I was thrilled and honoured to be part of Clive's special evening and to meet his clients. More than anything, it was so wonderful to see and feel how much love they have for him. It was beautiful to see."

For further information, please contact:

Clive Thompson

ENDS

Clive later said to me,

"Looking back, I learned so much from the first event that helped me when planning the second one.

I remember you saying the magic occurs after the talking when the wine flows and guests get to mix and mingle. I discovered in both events that some clients actually knew each other but neither knew they were working with Serenity.

I loved the "community" feel we'd created. Following your advice, I chose a quirky venue next to Lincoln Cathedral and a time of year when we could go outside to the 'secret garden' - a walled garden overlooked by the Cathedral.

Throw in a live musician (an acoustic guitarist) and we had a fabulous atmosphere. Loved doing it!"

Quite apart from anything else, such news makes great content for an adviser's website, reminds clients that you host events and helps your site to be picked up in Google search results.

In reality, much of what you tell the press will never end up in their publication, but what you are really doing here is building relationships, so that when something significant happens in the wider community or the country at large (for example, The Budget), who are your local (or even national journalists) going to turn to? Yes, people and businesses with whom they have a relationship.

And even if your press releases don't end up in a publication, add them to the News page on your website where they might get picked up by others, or indeed Google.

Don't underestimate the importance of PR – when handled well it can make a huge difference to the success of your promotional effort.

PR Quick Tips

- Make sure that your target market and prospects already engage (listen, view, read etc.) with the media outlet you are contacting.

- Don't know what media outlets to contact? Try asking your existing clients what papers or magazines they read and news outlets they engage with, and then write to them.

- Make sure that you send your press release to the right journalist. Many newspapers and magazines have a catch-all email address for press releases, so do some research to find out the name and contact details of the most appropriate journalist on their team.

- Include a powerful headline so that you get their attention. Write out several different titles for your release and choose the one that you feel will hit the spot. If in doubt, ask your colleagues for their ideas too.

- When sending content to the press, try to mirror their style – particularly their headlines. For example, if they are serious in tone, then write your release in the same style. If they are more sensational in approach, then adapt your release accordingly.

- When writing your media release, it's obviously important to get your key points and messages across, but try to do it within a story and make an emotional connection with the journalist and his/her readers. Case studies are a great way to do this.

- Even though making an emotional connection is important in your press release, don't take too long to get to the point. The first paragraph must make a key point.

- If possible, try to include numbers in your press release – particularly those that support what you are trying to say. For example, if you are running an event as a result of some customer feedback or a survey that you have run, include the headline numbers that support the point you are making.

- Try to ensure that your press release covers off the key areas of who, what, when, where and why. For example, what is happening, where and when is it happening, why is it happening and who is (or was) involved?

- Include at least one quotation within your press release which supports the story you are telling. For example, this from Serenity's press release:

'Clive commented, *"This event was everything I'd hoped it would be and more. Not only were my clients able to learn more about Financial Life*

> *Planning and our business, they were able to meet several members of the Serenity Team…"*

- Include a photo of yourself and/or the person quoted within your press release.

- Avoid overuse of financial jargon and keep your sentences short and to the point. Avoid waffle because many journalists receive multiple press releases every day.

- Remember to include your contact details so that the journalist can get back to you. Give them choices – such as email, phone, Twitter etc.

- Aim to keep your release to one side of paper. Two is OK but one is much better and makes it quicker and easier for the journalist to absorb.

  If you have a lot more information that you feel should be included, provide it on your website via a link in the press release.

- Proofread it before sending it off to make sure that there are no spelling mistakes or grammatical errors.

- End your release with "ENDS". This shows journalists that you are familiar with how publications and press releases work.

General Office Correspondence

However much of an expert you are and however good your local reputation, you still need to get people to attend your event. This means pulling out all the stops.

Even within the context of carefully planned promotions, it is still important to constantly wear your marketing hat and look out for every possible opportunity to tell people about your event.

Make absolutely sure that your seminars are mentioned in some shape or form on **everything** that leaves your office or premises. For example:

- If you have franking machine where the logo and message can be customised, change it to include the title of your seminar, or the date, or the details of a page on your website which has further information.

- Print brief details as above on your envelopes, or even make up some stickers which can be affixed to your envelopes.

- Make up a special batch of your notepaper which includes brief details of your seminars. Do the same with your compliments slips.

- Make up some special business cards which highlight your seminar prominently or add a message on the reverse of your current cards.

- Have a selection of 'giveaways' like pens, mugs, T-shirts, mouse mats, umbrellas, golf balls, coasters etc. printed with very brief details of your seminar: e.g. Post-It notepads can be personalised with your own artwork, photos and designs.

- Have rear window stickers printed for your car with details of your seminars or your website. They are available in a wide range of sizes and designs. They are incredibly cheap and will be seen by literally thousands of people in your local area and beyond.

- If you drive a 4x4 vehicle, you could have a spare wheel cover made up which promotes your company or events. Again, these are generally inexpensive and available in metal, vinyl or plastic.

- Print leaflets about your seminars which visitors to your shop or office premises can take away with them. Include one in every piece of correspondence that you send out.

- Add a link to information about your seminar in your email signature.

- Finally, make sure that people who call you out of hours are still given details. Re-record your answerphone message to include brief details, or direct them to either call your mobile phone or to visit your website.

The object of all this is to *get people to attend your seminars and workshops*. They will only do this though if they can see that there is something of real value to be gained from attending. If they can see that, they will gladly attend and will even pay to do so.

So it follows that all your promotional activities must be distinctive and make the benefits absolutely clear. Remember, when someone sees an advertisement of any description which appears to be targeting them, they will subconsciously say *"What's in it for me?"*

In short:

- Tell them what is in it for them
- Spell out all the benefits
- Offer them an incentive or a discount for booking immediately or in bulk
- Find an excuse for giving them a discount anyway
- Offer them valuable bonuses, to reassure them that they have made the right decision

Above all, get help from other people to promote your events and also offer them incentives for doing so. A great way of getting help is by using the incredible power of the internet...

ONLINE PROMOTION

First, your Website

When I initially wrote this book in 2003, what follows below are the first two paragraphs that began this section. I've kept them in the 2019/2020 version to show you how much things have changed since then. Indeed, looking back over the first edition, I'm amazed how little I referred to use of the internet to promote your seminars, workshops and live marketing initiatives.

Here's what I wrote:

"If this book was being written in the early part of the 1990s, many in small UK businesses would consider this section somewhat of a fantasy. Yet just a few years later [2003] the internet is now firmly part of our lives – to the extent that Internet Service Providers (ISPs) now enable us to keep a live connection 24 hours a day.

But as we have seen, the majority of small businesses in the UK are not yet using the internet for e-commerce purposes to anything like the extent they could. In fact, there are some industries in the UK which have yet to grasp the true potential offered by the worldwide web. This is disappointing, that they have much to look forward to!"

Every year I host multiple seminars and events – some free, some chargeable (depending on my objectives for the event concerned). But despite the wealth of promotional methods that I have already listed in this book, today it is entirely possible to promote successful and profitable events using *only* the internet.

But this is important - *all* of the offline promotional methods I have highlighted still work very effectively – the secret today is to adapt them to the online space. And when you have a promotional strategy which combines *both* offline and online, then real magic happens.

'Online' covers a multitude of sins, so let's start with your website.

The simple fact of the matter is, that most people and businesses promoting seminars and live marketing events will default to using their website and social media – despite the fact that everything you have read so far about offline marketing is proven to work.

So why will we inevitably default to using the internet?

For the simple reason that we perceive it to be easier and have greater reach. After all, who in their right mind wants to spend all that time on writing mailing letters, building a Dream 100 and doing all this old school marketing...

So, I get it that most of us are going to want to take the perceived easy route to getting bums on seats.

Unfortunately, all too often businesses default to the internet and then wonder why only half of the tickets end up being booked.

And you would be forgiven for thinking that the internet will do all of the hard work for you – what with amazing event tools at our disposal like Eventbrite, TicketSource, Ticket Tailor, Eventzilla, Cvent, RegOnline, Facebook's event tool, LinkedIn's new event tool, XING Events and several others – not to mention Twitter, Instagram and other social media tools.

It's easy to forget that, just like your website these are merely tools to help people make the decision to book up. Yes, to some extent these platforms will find potential attendees for you, but they will be useless unless someone actually finds your event listing, likes what they see and decides to attend.

So once again we come back to the basics of attracting people to attend your event:

- Having a great offer
- Targeting a niche
- Identifying your target market's needs and problems

- Highlighting how you solve them
- Bonuses and incentives
- Fantastic copywriting

Without these key ingredients, even the best event platform or website will still fail to fill your seminar room.

Designing your Event Page

There are two schools of thought as to how you should design the web page that will be promoting your event.

Neither is right nor wrong, but you should choose the approach that will have most appeal to your target audience. Put yourself firmly in their shoes.

Option 1: Full Length Sales Page

Create a sales page that is the online equivalent of your mailing letter.

This can either be on your existing website or on a separate dedicated site or landing page. Either way it needs to have a domain that makes sense to people when they find it – such as www.jonesandcoIFA.com/events or www.jonesandcoIFA.com/seminars. You might even want to use a dedicated domain such as www.jonesandcoIFAevents.com. It's entirely up to you.

However you do it, **the sole purpose of this page should be to sell your event**, and there should be no other links that could distract people from the task at hand. I wouldn't even have a link to Home or to anywhere that could distract and encourage visitors to leave the page.

As I mentioned a moment ago, this is a sales page so needs to include everything that we have discussed previously that will take people to their tipping point where they make the decision to attend.

Therefore, this is not the time to miss anything out. By reading the text on this page they need to see:

- The backstory of why this event is being held

- What's in it for them

- The exact benefits of attending

- How attending will improve their lives

- How others have benefited who have attended previously or who have worked with you

- Testimonials (ideally on video) from previous attendees or clients of yours

- What it will cost (if appropriate)

- Incentives for attending – such as discounts

- Bonuses for attending – such as additional value over and above the content of your event

- Location, date and time

- Whether overnight accommodation is available

- How easy it is to get to the venue and location of nearby travel hubs – including maps

- What else is nearby that might tempt them to make a longer trip of it

- Detailed information about the speaker(s), their backstory and why they/you are the right person to be presenting at the event

- Information about any charitable or philanthropic activities running alongside the event

- Can they bring a guest

- What is the refund policy

- Will there be food and refreshments

- The dress code

- How they can ask questions before they make a decision to attend

Don't be afraid to write a long sales page, because people want this level of detail. Far too many seminar hosts think they need to keep their sales page (or mailing letter for that matter) short, and so often miss out on providing the level of detail that people want. Remember, every little detail on your sales page will help to nudge people closer to their personal tipping point.

Ideally you should hire a professional copywriter, but this can be expensive – though you may be able to find a student at a local college or university who is studying marketing or creative writing who could help you with this. Maybe you have your own marketing team, in which case they will be fine.

However, it is important to remember that this is a sales page, and whilst it needs to be informative, it also needs to sell your event. So there are a couple of things you can do:

Firstly, write your copy for the sales page and then show it to three or four people who you might be targeting. Explain to them that you are putting on the event and invite them to share their opinions on your promotional materials – perhaps even offering them a free ticket in exchange for their help.

This goes back to what I was saying earlier by getting help from other people. Many will be only too willing to work with you.

Secondly, there are now software packages that can literally write your sales page for you! And after you have used such software a few times, it needs very little human input and tweaking afterwards.

Not only will it write the sales copy for your promotional page, it can also write advertisements that you can post on social media, headlines for mailers and emails and even PowerPoint slides. Does that sound good?!

I have seen several of these software packages over the years, but my favourite by a long way is Funnel Scripts – created by leading copywriting expert Jim Edwards. It is not cheap, but the value you get from it is incredible because it can be used in many different situations in your wider business and will pay for itself many times over.

Take a look at my resources page at www.philipcalvert.com/resources or send me an email at philip@philipcalvert.com.

To summarise, with this page on your website you are selling your event and it is literally the online version of what you would write in a mailing letter.

At the end of the page should be your call to action, where people can book there and then and pay for their ticket if your event is chargeable.

Create your Irresistible Offer

Do not forget to include your value stack on your promotional page as described earlier, where you list out all the incentives and bonuses that you are providing for attendance – along with their value.

Don't underestimate the importance of doing this because, whilst first and foremost you are promoting a ticket to your event, and good as your event is going to be, we need to make it **irresistible**. And you do this by creating an offer they can't refuse.

To do this you have to be constantly thinking about what's in the event for your audience – and it goes much further than just great content.

Your offer could be (for example):

- Powerful content that could change their lives

- Proven speakers who are (the) experts on the topic
- A stunning venue
- Great food and refreshments throughout the event
- Video and audio recordings of the event
- A valuable handout which includes additional materials
- Time for their personal questions to be answered
- Access to and use of the hotel's spa
- A fantastic networking opportunity
- The opportunity to bring a friend or guest
- Membership of your private Facebook or LinkedIn group
- A copy of your book
- A copy of your Tips Guide or Cheat Sheet
- A copy of your twenty-page report on how to solve XYZ problem
- Access to a follow up webinar
- A wine tasting after the event

- Access to additional resources online that are only available to attendees

- Access to your online course

Do you see what we are doing here? We are taking other things you can include and adding them in as a valuable bundle or package.

Yes, you are promoting a place at your event, but by including all this extra value, you are turning it into an irresistible offer. The more targeted to the specific needs and problems of your target market, the better and the more valuable and attractive they will perceive the offer to be.

Front of mind of everyone reading your promotional materials (whether offline or online) is always *"What's in it for me?"*, so make it easy for them to see exactly what they will get and how they will benefit so they have little choice but to sign up. Your overall offer is everything.

What is *not* an offer?

- The fact that you are a family business
- The fact that you have been in business for a hundred years
- The fact that your focus is local
- The fact that you have won awards for your product or service
- The fact that you have 'CFP' after your name
- The fact that you are a firm of Chartered Financial Planners

Do you see the difference?

The points that I have just listed are great and something to be proud of, but they do not constitute an offer.

So here's the thing – if you are getting traffic to your promotional page on your website and people are not purchasing or booking tickets, then your offer isn't yet good enough.

That's not the end of the world – simply tweak your offer until people start signing up. But again, you should test your offer in advance by talking to a few people in your target market to see what they think about your offer. And if in doubt, ask them what they would like to see in your overall offer that would swing it for them.

Sometimes you will need to come up with several offers until people start signing up. So make it easier for yourself - don't assume, ask instead. And that too is another reason why you need to take five months planning and promoting your events.

Option 2: Squeeze Page

As an alternative to a full-length sales page with a call to action at the bottom, you can use a squeeze page.

A squeeze page is also known as a landing page but is usually very much shorter and with very little text or content – but what there is, has a great deal of focus. It is the complete opposite to Option 1 we described earlier.

Usually the focus of the page addresses the primary problem or issue faced by your target market and then offers a solution in exchange for an email address. The solution is usually provided in the form of an instantly downloadable eGuide, eBook, report or even a video.

In the context of promoting your forthcoming seminar or event, your squeeze page fulfils a couple of roles.

To get the attention of your target market

If you are hosting a seminar aimed at a specific target market and they arrive on your page, it needs to make them feel that they are in the right place. It may be that they saw an advertisement for your event on Facebook, in a newspaper or magazine or perhaps in a LinkedIn post, and when they visit the quoted link, they are already a warm lead.

The fact that they are warm to your promotion will make it much more likely that they will keep reading.

To offer them free value immediately

Your initial promotion or advertisement has led them to your squeeze page, so we need to keep their attention by immediately offering them something for free that appears to show that you a) understand their needs and problems and b) which has the potential to ease or even solve those issues.

Let's imagine that you are someone in their sixties who has been hearing about the need to plan for their later life care – or perhaps increase their income. You have read about later life financial planning, so the subject is on your radar.

You subsequently hear from a local financial adviser – perhaps through a radio interview, blog or mailshot, that they will be hosting a seminar next month on the subject. You follow the link quoted and arrive on the adviser's squeeze page.

The text on the page is short and to the point and there are no distractions to lure you away. The text reads:

Are you concerned that you might run out of money in retirement and have nothing for your personal care?

Get our free guide now and discover our best twenty tips on how to keep your home and loved ones secure. Get instant access by entering your name and email address here...

Because later life financial planning was already on your radar, it makes it very likely that you won't hesitate to exchange your email address for further information from a local expert.

The squeeze page may also include a really short video of the adviser him or herself introducing themselves and reiterating the problem that you and many like you are facing. At this stage the video makes no mention of the forthcoming seminar and only has focus on the issue at hand – offering a free, high quality eGuide with answers to your questions.

That is all the squeeze page should seek to do. When the visitor enters their email address, their guide is either emailed to them automatically or they can download it from the second page.

At this point you, the financial adviser have a couple of choices.

You now have someone who has told you that they are potentially in the market for even more information, and whilst one option is to contact them directly, another is to show them how they can get that information – at your seminar next month.

The fact that they have freely given you their email address makes it much more likely that they will be inclined to want to attend, so that second page could be the longer promotional copy that we talked about earlier and which gives them the option to sign up there and then.

If they don't sign up there and then, you are able to communicate with them through email over the next few days and weeks.

That second page need not be the longer promotional page; it could just be a thank you page where they download their guide, and you then use their email address to follow up carefully and professionally over the coming days.

Typically you will want to ask them if they got their download and whether they have any questions that were not covered. You can then quite legitimately make mention of your forthcoming seminar (which may or may not be chargeable).

The point is, the visitor is now on your value ladder. They have:

- Seen an article or advertisement about you
- Visited your squeeze page

- Made a micro commitment by freely giving you their email address in exchange for some value and expertise
- Been made aware of your forthcoming event

I would argue that this person is now a 'client'. True, not a client as a financial adviser might typically define one, but they are definitely someone who has made a small commitment to engaging with you. And if they like and value the information you have given them in the form of the eGuide, then it makes it very much more likely that they will proceed to the next step.

It is the small commitment which is all important, but as you can see from this example, it is a risk-free commitment. And when they can see that it was a risk worth taking, then they begin to get to know you, get a sense of your expertise and credibility and most of all start to build trust in you.

I should add at this stage that when they enter their email address to access the eGuide, you should include a box that they tick which states that they understand that you will keep their email address strictly private, that you promise not to spam them and that they agree to receive further information about the topic concerned.

Let's summarise what's happened.

- You have identified a market you want to target through a seminar or live event.

- You have created specific objectives for your event - objectives for you and your business and objectives for your attendees.

- You have pinpointed that market's issues and problems – solutions to which you have and which you will share at your event.

- You have promoted your event offline and online.

- You have created dedicated web pages to which people can respond (in addition to traditional response methods they can use such as paper-based reply slips, email etc.).

- On visiting your web pages, visitors will be met with either a targeted sales message followed by the opportunity to sign up – or they will see a squeeze page which gets right to the heart of their issue and which offers them a free eGuide or solution there and then.

- You now have an email address with which to follow up in a professional and non spammy manner.

Hopefully you can now see what's happening here. We are metaphorically trying to 'meet people at the door', take them by the hand, empathise with them and guide them to the solution.

The first part of that solution is your eGuide. It's potentially highly valuable to them, and after it has built initial trust with the client, the next logical step for them to take is to attend your event – particularly if the offer is irresistible.

In the early days of using websites to promote events, we didn't take this 'hand-holding' approach and it was all about doing everything we could to hold (trap) them on our site. And we did that by just bombarding them with information in a vain attempt to make our site 'sticky'. Do you remember web designers telling you that your site needed to be 'sticky'?

That was the problem – visitors got stuck in our website, got confused with all the information and then left.

Unfortunately, many of our websites are still like that, and far too many website designers continue to peddle the idea. 'Busy' websites only serve to confuse visitors with multiple links that send people all over the place. I recently looked at one hundred financial advisers' websites and on average counted thirty-four clickable links on the home page alone.

If you are going to use a website to help promote and encourage people to sign up to your event, then the pages concerned need to totally focus on the job at hand. They need to take the visitor by the hand and lead them to the solution to their problem.

This approach is known as a funnel and is ideal for event promotion. Your own web designer can create a funnel for you, but here are several easy-to-use software packages that offer ready-made funnels that you simply model and adapt to your particular project. Current tools include:

- ClickFunnels
- Infusionsoft
- LeadPages
- Unbounce
- OptimizePress
- BuilderAll
- Kartra
- Plus many others

For most of these you don't need any special coding skills, and you literally drag and drop the elements you need to create your funnel.

You might also want to plug in email automation tools so that you can respond to people automatically, but if you are using funnel software just to promote a seminar or event, you can manage emails manually in your normal system (Gmail Outlook etc.).

My personal favourite is ClickFunnels and I can create squeeze and sales pages in a matter of minutes. Take a look at my resources page where you can get a free trial. www.philipcalvert.com/resources

Use Powerful and Proven Words and Phrases

Within your promotional text on the long sales page, make sure to use powerful, emotive words and phrases like:

- How to
- Discover
- Proven
- Secrets of
- Revealed
- We reveal
- Easy steps
- Special formula
- Profits
- You
- Free

Think carefully about the headings and titles on your sales page(s). Take a leaf out of some of these proven headings and model them to suit your own business, products and services:

- The X Most Effective Strategies for…
- X Steps to Achieve…
- X Ways to Y Without…
- X Ways to Increase Your Chances of…
- X Things to Consider When…
- Why Doing X Every Day Makes You More…
- The X Questions You Need to Ask Before…
- X Rules You Must Follow if You Want to…
- X Critical Things You Didn't Know about…
- X Strategies/Tips/Tools to Get You _____ Results Fast
- The X Mistakes that Are Costing You…
- A Simple Way to X That Will Work for Any…
- The Ultimate Guide for People Who Want to _____ But Can't Seem to Get Started
- Your X Biggest Questions About Y Answered

…and so on.

There are literally hundreds of permutations on headlines and headings like this and you can find many more with a Google search. Again, software tools like Funnel Scripts can help you to create your own.

When creating headlines and headings within your promotional text, try to anticipate every question which people may wish to ask you either before attending or during the event itself and answer them within the body of the text.

You may also wish to put the text in the form of a Frequently Asked Questions list or even interview with you, where all the relevant questions asked.

This is important because when people read your promotional materials, in addition to asking themselves *"What's in it for me?"*, they will also be subconsciously coming up with objections, so try to pre-empt them in your text.

Correct Positioning of Incentives on the Page

We mentioned earlier that it is important to offer incentives and bonuses. Put these towards the end of the page after you have already given people at least three opportunities to click on a link which takes them to your booking form.

Some people will go to the booking form/page at the first opportunity and won't even see the bonus that they will receive until they read it all again later (which they will). Remember, the bonuses are really there to confirm in people's minds that they are

a) going to get high value content at your event and

b) to reassure them that they have made the right choice in deciding to attend – so list these bonuses (and their value) near or at the end of the text *after* you have been through the main benefits of attending in detail.

And c) to create an irresistible offer.

Provide Choices

As mentioned earlier, provide people with a wide range of options to find out further information from you or to book tickets.

If you are charging for attendance you must also provide a wide range of payment options, including secure credit card facilities. If you do not have such facilities, again these are available from a number of providers and are ridiculously easy to integrate to your site.

A popular facility is provided by PayPal and is ideal for businesses which are gradually building e-commerce strategy. The set-up is free and all you pay is very small percentage of each transaction, which is deducted by PayPal at source. PayPal is extremely good value and ideal to small businesses wanting to trade online. Stripe is another good option.

Extra Online Tips to Attract People to your Seminars

Of course, despite your best efforts, not every visitor to your site is going to find your event completely irresistible, so you need to put in place a few tricks to try to hold them at the exit and reduce the likelihood that they will leave.

Firstly, get the hygiene factors in place, the most important of all being to know your numbers. Check your site stats to see how many visitors you are getting, how long they stay etc. and how many of them either download your guide or register for your event.

Another hygiene factor is to split test both your squeeze page and the page with longer copy. This means creating different versions of both pages and comparing results from each. Either your website designer can do this or in some cases the funnel software you use can create split test versions.

When the stats show you which of your pages is performing best, then you can safely delete the other. If you want to, you can then create another page and monitor the stats from that one with a view to deleting the page that performs least well. Professional internet marketers continually split test their web pages until they get to a point where performance can't be improved upon.

Pop-ups

Like them or not, pop-ups have their place. Use them professionally so that when someone moves to leave your promotional page without taking any action, you have another option to engage with them.

Don't simply repeat the promotion that is already on the web page, but add something of value to your offer – and make it something they can access immediately.

There are two objectives for the pop-up:

- To convince people that your seminar *really is* worth attending and that if they book today, they will receive *additional* valuable bonuses.

    These could be free samples of your main product, a free book, or perhaps a free five- or seven-day email course giving them short tips and advice on something related to your business – but which will be of real value to them.

In short, if they book now, they will get even more value.

- The second objective of the pop-up is to get people to leave their email address.

    You may want to give someone a free 'information product' just for visiting your website, but they can only get it by email so they have to leave you their address.

Countdown Clocks and Progress Bars

Including a countdown clock near the sign-up button or registration form is a proven way to promote a sense of urgency to the site visitor.

Rather than use it to 'scare' people into signing up quickly by saying the price will go up in the next five minutes, the best way to incorporate a countdown clock is to offer additional bonuses if they sign up immediately – i.e. add more value to the offer. Remember – adding value as often as possible is the way to go.

Progress bars are another popular tool that internet marketers use to visually show visitors and potential purchasers that the sign-up process is almost complete, and thus encourages them to stay the distance.

Testimonials

Wherever possible include testimonials from people who have either attended a previous event or who are existing clients. Ideally these should be video testimonials and the best ones are those recorded immediately after your event has finished.

Some of the most effective event promotions I have seen are where video testimonials are up front and central on the website. They don't need to be professionally produced – your mobile phone camera will be fine – but do make sure that the sound is clear. Purchase a simple clip on microphone that plugs into your phone and it will make all the difference. You can get these for next to nothing online.

When filming video testimonials, aim to follow this formula by asking your interviewee to say:

- Who they are and what they do
- What they got out of your event or working with you – plus the results they have seen
- What they would say to others who are thinking of hiring you or attending a future event of yours

Your recording need only be short; sixty to ninety seconds maximum will be fine.

It is really important that you make a point of planning for your interviews. Sometimes it can be a little chaotic immediately after your event – particularly if it has gone well and attendees want to talk to you, so allocate the job of getting interviews to a friend or someone on your team so that the opportunity is not missed to get people's reactions while they are still 'warm'.

Make Better use of your Email Newsletter

Whilst your email newsletter is a great way to keep the relationship plates spinning with your clients and prospects, it is also an excellent vehicle for finding material for your seminars.

A great way to keep in touch *and* interact with people is to run regular surveys with your clients and indeed people who are not yet clients.

Ask questions related to your industry and find out what problems people have. For example, a financial adviser could ask clients what their main concerns are about their finances. You might find that 70% of people say that they are worried about not having enough money to live on in retirement. This will give you a good clue as to what to include in your seminars.

Build up a database of problems and prepare solutions accordingly, either for delivery at your seminars, or for written, audio or video form. As mentioned earlier, put your conclusions and solutions in articles for the local press, or write special reports which you give away as an incentive for attending your seminar. You could even sell these reports on your website.

Your material and intellectual property is key to the success of your seminars, not just for promotional purposes, but also as a generator of income in its own right. The choice of how you package this information and subsequently use it is yours – the key is getting it in the first place.

People attend seminars and workshops because they want information on something that is either of general interest or very close to their heart. Very often that information will help them in some way. If you can find out what sort of problems people have or information they would like in advance, you are then able to make the content of your seminars very much more appealing. And your email newsletter is an excellent way of obtaining that information.

And clearly, email is a powerful tool with which to promote your seminars. However, you need to be very careful about the words and phrases that you use in your emails, because spam filters can catch you out.

Typically words such as these in your emails could prevent them from being delivered to your prospects:

- No credit check
- Once in a lifetime
- Work at home
- Take action now
- Congratulations!
- Expect to earn
- Additional income
- Clear your debts
- Free mobile phone
- Attention homeowners
- No catch
- Dear friend
- Financial freedom
- Lose weight
- Pure profit
- Be your own boss
- Compare rates
- Stop snoring
- Click to remove

These are fairly extreme examples, but I've included them here to encourage you to think carefully about the words and phrases you might use in your own email newsletter and seminar promotions.

You can probably guess a lot more words and phrases that are picked up by spam filters, but the difference between emails which contain these words and your own, is that spam emails are generally trying to get you to part with your money.

The good news is that your email is unlikely to use many of these words because you are not trying to sell. In fact, you are giving – giving valuable information which people have asked for. If you are worried about whether your email newsletter is at risk of being caught by filters, there are a variety of online services which will analyse your text and provide you with a report before you hit the send button.

A better approach in email marketing is to approach people as if you are telling them an anecdote in a pub – tell short, observational stories instead, which lead to you making a point that has relevance to the content of your events.

Many professional email marketers send out messages every day to their list. You would be forgiven for thinking that this would just irritate people, but whilst they do get unsubscribers, all the evidence shows that regular email communications which add value through storytelling are the most effective in building relationships and which ultimately lead to sales.

When to Send your Email Promotions

This is not an exact science, but it is generally believed by internet marketers that the best time to send emails is 10am on Tuesdays, because apparently this is the time when we are most open to receiving promotional emails.

From my own perspective, I tend to send promotions by email on either of Tuesday, Wednesday or Thursday mornings. On Mondays, recipients are too busy to take notice and on Fridays they are winding down mentally. Whilst most people use email 24/7 these days, there are still many who don't go near their inbox at weekends, so by Monday or Tuesday your email promotion is 'old news'.

What is important is that you get some consistency into the sending of your email newsletter, so that it ideally arrives at the same time every week. That way, recipients tend to expect it to be in their inbox. Internet psychologist Graham Jones is a prolific blogger (and has been for many years), but what I've noticed about Graham is that his newsletter arrives at the exact same time every week. Graham sends his on Saturdays, but because he is ruthlessly consistent in his approach, I read it every week. In fact, when I get Graham's weekly email newsletter it reminds me that all is well because the weekend is here.

Use their Name

It's a small point but use people's name in your email communications. This makes what might be a bulk email communication, look and feel more personal.

Also use their name in the body of the email – particularly the title. With modern email software it's pretty easy to do these days.

I also recommend using their name again towards the end of the final paragraph of your email, because as they read through your text, they can see their name out the corner of their eye, and this encourages them to keep reading.

Remember the personal tipping points we talked about earlier? Using someone's name could be the one thing that helps them to reach their tipping point where they commit to attending.

"Just a quick note to tell you about…"

Don't use the word "just" in your emails. Whilst it loosens the formality of an email message, it also has the effect of downplaying the importance of your message.

Instead, use something like *"I'm excited to tell you about…"* or *"I'm keen to tell you about…"*, or perhaps *"Clients have been asking me about…"*. You get the idea.

Use Video Email

Earlier I briefly referred to the use of video email, and I would like to expand on its importance here, because it can make a huge difference to the degree to which potential seminar attendees will engage with you.

You can't go anywhere on social media today without seeing more and more people talking direct to their friends, prospects and customers using video – often on Facebook and increasingly on LinkedIn and Instagram.

It is incredibly engaging, and that's why the likes of Facebook rewards its use because it helps to keep people on their site.

Firstly, on the promotional pages for your event on your website, you should also use video because it will help to hold people there – and it gives viewers an opportunity to see the whites of your eyes and get to know you – much like your seminar itself.

But what you see far less of is people using video in emails, and that surprises me. In many ways it doesn't surprise me because very few people know that you can even send video emails. But when you do, it has exactly the same effect as when you use it on social media or on your website.

Here are just a few benefits of using video in your emails:

- You stand out in your audience's crowded inbox
- You connect at a human level with your recipients
- It gives people a glimpse into your personality
- It empowers your greatest asset – you
- Face to face relationships get results
- It differentiates you from your competition

What's not to like?!

So here is how you could use this technology:

- Send video email newsletters every week instead of text based, or send both with the video at the top above the text.

- Send automated, but preferably personalised video emails to thank people for signing up to your seminar.

- Send video emails to remind people about your seminar a couple of days before the date of your event.

- Send video emails to send personalised answers to questions asked at your event – or to expand on answers you gave at the time.

- Send video emails to thank people for attending.

And yes, you can also use video emails as part of your day to day business communications throughout the year. It may be that you are in a business where you rarely meet your customers or clients, but by sending them the occasional personalised video message instead of the usual text based email, it helps them to get to know the face behind the name, and that in itself could be enough to encourage them to attend your next event.

I'm aware of several businesses who now use video emails to onboard new clients into their service.

We are only limited by our own imaginations as to how we use video email in our businesses. It may feel a bit awkward at first getting used to a new way of communicating, but it doesn't take long to get the hang of it.

My video email platform of choice is BombBomb, which you can find at https://bombbomb.com. Another useful tool is Bonjoro at www.bonjoro.com

Use Social Proof

Humans, being social animals, will often copy each other's behaviour. And where we can see that others like us have behaved in a certain way, it makes it very much more likely that we will also act in the same way.

You can use this to your advantage when promoting your events, by showing video testimonials and comments from people who have either worked with you or attended a previous event.

If you can also show on your website that people are booking tickets to your event, this increases the likelihood that others will too. A great tool to do this is Morevago which randomly displays reviews or recent bookings on your promotional page.

Morevago claim that on average, their users see a 34% increase in new customers from their website in only 30 days, simply by installing their simple tool. I use this tool myself and can vouch for its effectiveness.

Take a look at www.morevago.com where there is currently a fourteen-day free trial.

Don't underestimate the power of Social Proof in your seminar promotions, because it will be a key driver in moving people towards their tipping point where they make the decision to attend. If they can see through your promotional materials, that *other people like themselves* are getting X results from working with you or attending your events, then that will be a big factor in their decision-making process.

In addition to Social Proof, where we look to other's behaviour to point us the way, there are several other factors that influence human behaviour, including:

Reciprocation – where we feel obliged to return favours. This is one of the reasons why we include bonuses and incentives in our promotions.

Authority – we are naturally drawn to experts in an area where we have interest. Hence one of the reasons for including a detailed personal profile as part of our promotions.

Commitment and Consistency – where we want to act in accordance with our personal values. Hence the need for us to have a full understanding of our target market and reflecting that in our promotions.

Scarcity – where we fear missing out. Think about how we can introduce scarcity into our promotions – perhaps through limited availability of places at the event etc.

Likeability – we are naturally drawn to people we like. This is one of the reasons we put on seminars in the first place, because it gives people the opportunity to get to know, like and trust us. Remember the phrase 'People buy people'.

I am far from an expert on the psychology behind these factors, but I always use all of them in my own seminar and event promotions. In fact when you create a mailing letter or promotional web page for your events, you should make a point of cross checking against this list to ensure that you have included an element of each because it makes your promotion so much more persuasive.

If 'social influence' is of interest to you, I highly recommend that you look at *Influence – The Psychology of Persuasion* by Robert Cialdini.

Social Media

It is entirely possible to promote a seminar and fill the room using *only* social media – particularly if you have a clear niche target market. I have done it many times, but let's make it easy for ourselves by getting some focus into how we use social.

Jared Reynolds is a financial planner based in Columbia, Missouri whose niche market is men and women who enjoy bass fishing. This includes both professional bass fishermen and also entrepreneurs, business owners, accountants, lawyers – and indeed anyone who enjoys bass fishing.

Jared arranges a range of retreats and events specifically targeted at these people. And to be clear, these are all chargeable events which the clients/prospects pay for, and which ultimately take his relationships with them to a completely different level.

Jared knows *exactly* where his target market hangs out online. He knows where he can find them on Twitter, Facebook, LinkedIn and Instagram – so reaching them with his event promotions is far from difficult. In fact it couldn't be easier.

In addition to financial advisers, another of my own target markets is speakers, coaches and consultants – and I know exactly where they hang out on social media. I know which Facebook groups they have joined and also the communities on LinkedIn where they can be found. I also know what industry publications they read, what hashtags they use, which websites they frequent, which newsletters they receive, which podcasts they listen to and which conferences they attend – so I have no shortage of places where I can potentially reach them.

I have also created my own online groups for my target markets on Facebook, LinkedIn and Mighty Networks. I use these groups to study and learn what their big issues, concerns and problems are at any moment in time. Within these groups I run polls and ask questions, so I know exactly what they are thinking and talking about.

I also use the groups to ask them what events they might be interested in attending if I was to put on a seminar or workshop. A good way to do this is through polls, where I list around six or seven ideas of my own and then ask which they would be most interested in.

Want to get bums on seats in *your* target market? Then **ask them** what topics you should include.

Yes, you can also use social media to shout from the rooftops and some of it will doubtless hit your target market, but one of the problems about social media is that it is far too noisy and far too random. Sure, you can give your use of social promotions a bit more focus through the use of relevant hashtags, but if you want to quickly and easily reach your target market then make life easier for yourself and fish where the fish are.

I could write a whole book on how to use social media in your marketing, but I would much rather keep the focus on **what actually works for event marketers** – and my primary strategy is as outlined above – go niche and embed yourself in relevant online communities, ideally building your own.

That said, here are some general social media approaches that I have also found effective when promoting seminars and events:

- Use paid Facebook advertising, remembering to retarget people after they visit your event website pages.

- Create a Facebook event page.

- Use paid LinkedIn advertising.

- Publish long, detailed, in-depth articles on LinkedIn.

- Search for and follow hashtags on LinkedIn that are used by your target markets.

- Engage with comments that use that hashtag – i.e. draw attention to yourself.

- Create your own unique hashtag, using it across all your chosen social media channels.

- Encourage people to use your hashtag and thank them when they do.

- Encourage existing clients and your seminar attendees to tweet and post about your events – again thanking them for doing so.

- Get close to your 'Dream 100' on social media as discussed earlier and encourage them to support you.

- Use Instagram to post images taken at your events.

- Host your own podcast and build up a following.

- Host your own YouTube channel and post regular content around your expertise – occasionally showing your video testimonials.

- If you have additional speakers at your event, ask them to tell their own networks about it on social media, including your hashtag.

- Create ready-made graphical content or swipe files for your speakers, affiliates and supporters that they can use in their social posts.

- Use photos of attendees and speakers in your social updates.

- Feature relevant quotes from speakers who will be presenting. Tag those speakers in your post and they will more than likely reshare your post.

- Share teaser slides that will be used at your event.

- Tweet visuals of testimonials from previous events or clients.

- Ask people to tag a friend in their own social posts who they think could benefit by attending. Reward people for tagging others.

- Share behind-the-scenes content in the lead up to your event – perhaps showing you creating promotional content, visiting venues, meeting speakers or rehearsing your presentation.

- Host a pre-event webinar or Facebook live to build hype. Give discounts on the main event or additional bonuses to people who book after the webinar.

- Use live streaming on LinkedIn to build hype.

- Promote your events on your LinkedIn company page.

- Create a Showcase page on LinkedIn where the focus is only on your event.

- Include links to your event in your email signature.

- Take ideas from any of the above and incorporate them into Instagram stories (and indeed Facebook stories).

- Write regular blogs that answer questions that are commonly asked by your clients or seminar attendees.

- Repurpose those blogs into videos, podcast episodes, infographics etc.

Not all of these will be relevant to all seminar hosts but use those which you feel will be appropriate to your market and event. There are of course many other ways that you could use social media to promote your events, but the ones I have listed above have worked best for me and others.

It should go without saying that I strongly recommend planning your posts and content well in advance, and use tools such as TweetDeck, Hootsuite and others to queue up your posts. Again, given all the possibilities of how you could and should use social media, it's another reason why your full planning can take five months.

Feed your Fish

Continuing the fish theme, I think it's important to reiterate the need to be strategic about your social media efforts. The list of ideas above is really about you acting at a tactical level, yet it's extremely important to be strategic too.

I mentioned Jared at the beginning of this section whose focus is on arranging events for people interested in bass fishing. And remember, Jared is a financial adviser – a financial adviser who only wants to work with people who enjoy not only fishing, but bass fishing! Now that is a niche.

Jared knows all the social media tactics, but he knows better than most that 'tweet and hope' is not a strategy that will ever bear fruit.

All too often I have people saying to me something along these lines:

"Phil, we're planning our events and I see that Jones and Co are using Twitter, so we think we might give that a go. And John Smith is using YouTube to promote his business, so we think we might give that a go too. Also, Sue down the road is using LinkedIn quite a lot, so do you think we should give that a go?"

Guess what? 'Give that a go' is not, nor ever will be a strategy that has any hope of success. I haven't got a problem with an element of experimentation and trial and error, but if you are going to use social media, you must have a strategy that is written down and one that you commit to.

That's why I strongly advocate the community approach use by Jared. He knows his target market; he knows exactly where he can find them online and so makes life easy for himself when it comes to promoting his events.

Community is everything when it comes to using social media to promote events, and I liken it to having a fish tank.

Here's how I use it with one of my target markets – financial advisers.

My fish tank is my online community - a Facebook group, LinkedIn group or a group on Mighty Networks.

The fish in the tank are my financial adviser members. And if you keep fish, you need to feed them.

By feeding them, I mean that on a daily basis you need to sprinkle food into the tank – in this case tips, links, resources, videos, ideas etc. In other words, content that excites financial advisers.

On a Monday I feed my fish; they log in, swim around, consume the food and then go away.

On Tuesday, I feed my fish by posting more tips, links, news, insights and value. Again, the fish turn up, swim around, consume the content and then go away.

On Wednesday, I repeat the same thing – feeding my fish with content that helps them in their businesses.

But what happens if I forget to feed them on Thursday? Guess what, they still all turn up, because they have come to expect food at a certain time each day. So when they turn up on Thursday, they swim around, pick up scraps left over from the previous day – and then go about their business as before.

Now if I also forget to feed them on Friday, they still show up, and this time – just to stretch this analogy – they bring their own lunch with them which they share amongst one another. By this I mean they post their own tips, ideas, questions and content.

So what has happened is that we have created community by regularly sharing content which our target market loves – and indeed often finds quite addictive. I've had financial adviser members of my online groups tell me that they often visit the group multiple times per day. One said this week that my Facebook group *"...is the go-to place for high quality business development resources for financial advisers"*.

That's really exciting for me to hear, but I have deliberately created that way. And the proof of concept is that when I want to put on a training event, seminar or workshop for the financial advisers in my community, **it always sells out** when I include it within the 'food' that I sprinkle in the tank.

In short, this won't happen overnight, but start your own fish tank, by building community around your brand online. Facebook and LinkedIn groups are a great place to start – though my personal favourite is Mighty Networks, because there is no advertising, no distractions from your topics at hand and no algorithms telling members what to look at.

Internet marketers always tell you about the importance of building your email list – and that is fine. But if you also want to use social media to promote events, seminars and workshops, then build your list in the form of an online community that you regularly feed with great content that enriches their lives.

It's important to remember that you don't have to have a group/community with thousands of members. Start small and aim for your first twenty – then thirty until you reach your first hundred. And even at that level you will be well on your way to building a valuable community that responds positively to your content and promotions.

Start by inviting your existing clients to join your group, plus local businesspeople and friends that you know - and then also include membership of your group as a valuable bonus for attendance at your events.

Don't stop promoting

Even if you have got all your ducks in a row and have been planning and promoting your event for a full five months, there will always be some potential attendees who either leave things to the very last minute – or who don't get to see your marketing until the evening before.

It's not your fault or theirs – it's just the way it is. A lot of seminar hosts do their promotion, get X number of registrations and then take their foot off the gas. That's possibly OK if you have already got a full house, but on the assumption that you could do with one or two more people in the room, you should continue your marketing right up to the day itself.

On more than one occasion, I've been heading to the venue and received a tweet or text message from someone who literally only saw my marketing and promotions that morning. If I can, I will always make some space for them and they are usually extremely grateful. And if you are hosting a chargeable event, that's more revenue in the bank.

There is also a case for keeping your online marketing (website, blogs etc.) live *after* your seminar, because again, I've had people contact me one day after the event saying how gutted they are that they only just found out about it. Good news! Put them on the mailing list for your next event.

Keep your website promotion live and add a notice saying *'Sold Out! Please register for priority notification of our next event so that you don't miss out.'*

Once again, social proof and scarcity coming into play.

Summary

We said at the outset of this comprehensive chapter that there are a multitude of different ways to promote your seminars, and essentially they fall into two types – offline and online promotion.

The key is not to rely on any one type of promotion and to never assume you know how people want to receive information. Try to be strategic, split test, listen carefully to your clients and make notes of what works best in your market.

Where once someone might have seen an event advertised in a letter, on a leaflet or a poster and then responded, they can now use another medium to obtain additional information and often it is the combination of promotional media which makes the difference and drives them towards their personal tipping point. Know your numbers and closely observe your prospects' behaviours as they go through your sales funnel. Learn from what you see.

Provide your clients and prospects with incentives to book early or in volume; offer valuable bonuses for attending and make available a variety of different ways to respond to your seminar promotion. Take careful note of what combination of bonuses and incentives seems to hit the spot.

Get people to help you promote your events by giving them generous incentives. Whilst the internet and email are just two ways of promoting your events, they are potentially your greatest 'helpers'. Take advantage of their incredible reach and power.

I cannot stress enough the importance of regularly communicating with your target market and asking them what they would like to see included if you were to put on an event. All too often we guess what they would want, without actually asking them.

And finally, whilst I have hopefully given you a few ideas, don't forget occasional use of trial and error. But above all, keep the communication going with your clients and get feedback on what they like and don't like about your seminar or workshop offering.

Having successfully managed to get some people to attend, if you make a good job of the event itself, anything between 65% and 100% of attendees will want a meeting or further discussion with you.

After that it's up to you, but a 65% + take-up rate wouldn't be too bad would it?

~

"I think the most important thing for small business owners to do is listen to their clients. The best thing I did recently was a customer survey. It was done externally and professionally.

I gained so many insights from that survey. My clients really opened up and I was happy to get tough messages as well as praise. The insights and requirements helped to sharpen my business strategy. The picture presented by the survey was as important for me to know as the P&L."

Jacqui Harper MBE, Founder, Crystal Business Training

How to Dramatically Increase Your Profits from Seminars, Workshops and Live Events

This is where the fun begins and the profits start to roll in!

In my experience, financial advisers who run seminars and events, primarily do it to educate or thank existing clients – rather than as a means to raise awareness and to attract new clients.

What's more, they are missing out on using their events to increase profits. Indeed, the seminar itself has the opportunity to be a profit generating activity in its own right.

Most cigarette advertising of old was rarely designed to encourage people to start smoking, but to persuade smokers to change their variety. But small businesses do not have the luxury of a budget to spend on simply building brand awareness. If you run a small business, your marketing spend must work very much harder for you. Ideally, it should promote your business, ask for business and generate business in its own right.

Where businesses do host promotional workshops or seminars, financial gain from the events themselves is not normally the prime motivator for holding them. More often than not, such events are only put on to raise profile in the hope of increasing sales at a later date. To make matters worse, many small business owners believe that charging a fee for attendance will actually be a disincentive to people attending. In reality, this is not the case.

As we said earlier a sensible but worthwhile entry fee will not put off people from attending seminars in the small business market.

Providing Value

Indeed, if you are targeting your seminars at larger companies to obtain exposure to (say) HR directors, these companies have budgets to attend such events and will think nothing of paying in excess of £250 for a ticket, particularly if they believe that they are going to get real value for their money. And as we have said elsewhere in this book, you must provide real value.

This means that if you are demonstrating your 'secrets' in your particular trade, business or profession, the golden rule is that you must never hold anything back. If for example you make extra special, scented soaps that are known for their beautiful aroma, smoothness or skin enhancing properties and which have a special ingredient, your workshop must 'tell all'.

Do not give the audience the slightest impression that you are holding something back from them. The word 'secrets' is used here in a marketing context and gives the impression to potential buyers that they are going to discover something that only the professionals know, which in turn makes the product or service even more special to them.

As consumers, we love to know what goes on behind the scenes, whether it is how the special effects in films are done, celebrities' lifestyles, how magic tricks or illusions performed and so on. The revealing of secrets is irresistible to most of us and as such can be used to your advantage when marketing your seminars.

'Myth busting' is another great way to share information on a particular topic. For example, the equity release market is currently undergoing a revival in the UK, and I am aware of some later life financial planners who are going to run seminars which will seek to bust common myths about equity release.

Turning Talk into Profit

But the purpose of holding seminars or workshops should not be just to obtain publicity for your business or product. They can and should be used to create and build substantial profits in their own right. And even if you still only want publicity from your events, it is still possible to turn your talk into profit with little effort.

As we have said earlier, unless you have your own premises in which you can host a talk, you will inevitably have to budget for hiring a venue. But how much better would it be if the event could pay for itself several times over?

In Chapter 6 we looked at how to market your events. In this section we will take it a step further and show how to get even greater value from your marketing spend, to the extent that your marketing effort can create income in its own right.

The really big profits from seminars don't just come from your main product or service that you promote or highlight at your events. They predominantly come from:

- The perception of your expertise
- Your ability to repackage that expertise into new products and services
- Your ability to upsell to other products that people need

For example, everyone knows that an accountant is an expert on tax, but an accountant that gets on his or her feet, talks about how people can benefit from that expertise and who does so in public at a seminar, is deemed to be *more* of an expert.

The simple act of standing up at a seminar has the effect of raising the perception of your expertise. You may not actually be any more of an expert than the next accountant, but you are perceived to be so. And of course, perception is everything!

So just hosting a seminar in itself creates an environment for clients and potential clients that is more conducive to them placing business with you. This presupposes that you have half-decent presentation skills and in Part 2 we will show you how not to fall flat on your face when you are up there talking.

The Seminar Income Stream

It's how you use your expertise that determines how much extra profit you will make. Let's look at the income stream from a typical seminar.

Typically, a seminar in a good quality branded hotel in the UK with the target audience of 100 people will incur costs broadly as follows:

All day room hire	:	£500
Tea and coffee three times	:	£675
Buffet lunch	:	£1250
Total	:	£2,425

This works out at £24.25 per delegate and includes an overhead projector, screen and flip chart. If you want more than one flip chart, I suggest you go and buy your own so that you can use it again and again. Higher charges for items like this can be extortionate and will severely dent your profits.

Unless you live close to the hotel and can guarantee to be there at least two hours before your talk starts, you should also add on the cost of accommodation for yourself and any helpers. If you feel even slightly rushed or under pressure to get to the venue on time, it will affect you for the first two hours of your talk.

Different hotels will also give you a selection of lunch menus. Generally you can opt for the cheapest, because if the hotel is any good at all, you will get a decent enough spread to please most people. Unless the lunch is truly awful, it will not make any difference at all to your rating by attendees. They are, after all, attending for the content of your seminar, not the content of the sandwiches.

If on the other hand you are hosting a weekend boot camp or retreat, you will have more latitude on the quality of the meals, but generally you will be able to build in the extra costs as people who attend weekend events will pay considerably more for their ticket. More on this later.

So in this example, you need to find at least £24.25 from each attendee to break even. But of course, it's much more than that once you have included:

- Accommodation and meals for yourself and helpers

- Materials – decent paper and pens (most hotels give each delegate about six sheets of paper and a pencil!)

- Workshop materials – binders, workbooks etc.

- Display holders and stands – to dispense your leaflets and business cards

- Sweets and mints – Bring your own, hotel sweets are dreadful

- Additional, *new* flip chart pens – the hotels are always running out of ink

- A laser pointer, ruler, golf club or similar to point to the screen or flip chart

- Small prizes for when someone in the audience says something vaguely profound. Offer a combination of sweets and fruit. Whilst sweets are more fun, they can lower blood sugar levels over time, which can affect the concentration of delegates. The complex carbohydrates within (say) bananas are released gradually, keeping energy levels higher and longer

- You may also need to hire all bring your own projector and laptop

In addition, I give delegates a pad of Post-It notes, a fluorescent highlighter pen and tab index markers. If you can have these personalised with your business name, freephone telephone, email address and website details, then all the better, as they will further enhance their perception of your professionalism.

If you have decided to adopt seminar marketing as a key promotional strategy, then all these things can be budgeted for, but I would rather that my seminars or workshops were purely profit generating, rather than a cost to my business.

How to Cover the Cost of each Attendee

We have already talked about the benefits of charging entry fee, so let's now look at how we can pay the seminar bills and generate *additional* income.

To make extra profits, you need to generate extra income and it's fair to say that the normal rules of marketing apply equally to Seminar Selling. That is, if you put on a good show, there's a fair chance that an attendee will want to buy your main product or service. You also hope they will tell a friend, who will in turn attend your next seminar.

Even better is if the friend decides they too want to buy your main product or service. If they like what they get, they in turn will tell someone else, who hopefully will come to a future seminar and also buy your product, and so it goes on. This is called referral income.

So the total income from your seminar looks like this:

Total income (TI) = ticket sales income (TSI) + main product/service sales income (PSI) + referral income (RI)

But we know that TSI above will be £0 if we don't charge an entry fee, and PSI and RI are for the most part unknown (at least for the first few seminars you host).

What we need to do is find even more ways of creating income from your seminars. Here are a couple.

Consulting Income (CI)

By standing up in front of an audience, you are building an image of expertise. And before I go further, make absolutely sure you really are an expert on the subject concerned, or they will see through you. There is nothing worse that standing up in front of an audience who know more about the topic than you! Better still – try to be *the* expert on the subject.

Whilst the objective of your seminar may be to eventually sell more of your main product or service, there will be some people in the audience who feel there is more to learn from you before they purchase your product, or who wish to hire you as a consultant or coach on a regular basis. This creates your consulting income which is in addition to your main product or service income.

Additional Product Income (API)

There are huge extra profits to be made through the sale of other relevant materials *at and after* your seminars – either at the back of the room (BOR sales), by mail order or from your website. But it is BOR sales that are the key to turning your events from merely promotional activity to a high profit generating sales strategy.

An example of this approach is used in the film industry, where promotional merchandising can bring in a massive income on the back of the film itself. Indeed, some movies make more money from the merchandising than the film itself. Examples include:

- Toys
- Games
- Lunchboxes
- Tee-shirts
- Underwear
- Hats
- Posters
- Action figures
- Playing cards
- Bedding
- Candles
- Ties
- Online games
- Colouring books
- Drinks
- Diaries
- Calendars
- Pens
- Pendants
- And even the legendary Darth Vader Burger

Some business owners, particularly speakers, trainers and consultants find that this aspect of their business becomes so successful that they completely reengineer their business to focus purely on BOR and website sales. Whereas they started out offering consultancy and training, they often move into seminars where they then sell additional materials.

In some examples, their sales of additional materials have been so successful, they are then asked to speak for high fees on how they achieve that success. Naturally, they then sell more materials whenever they are asked to speak!

What could *you* sell in addition to your current service?

The list is endless and only limited by your imagination to create products. Here are some suggestions.

Books

Let's start with the big one – books. We have said that by standing up in front of a group of people, be they existing or potential customers, you are enhancing their perception of you is an expert.

Assuming you are an expert on your subject (and you wouldn't be in business if you weren't), there is no reason why you can't write down your knowledge. In other words, sit down and write a book.

Do your research and find out which publishers want your sort of material, learn how to write a book proposal or synopsis and get on with it. Expect some rejection but keep at it. For information on how to write a proposal, check out my book *56 New Income Streams for Financial Advisers: How to Turn your Financial Planning Expertise & Experience into Profitable Information Products for the Digital Age* at www.amazon.co.uk/dp/1689129816

Your own book is one of the best ways of enhancing the perception of your expertise credibility. People always prefer to listen to experts and if you have something in print, it subconsciously tells people that you really are an expert.

Writing a book is probably the hardest way to build an additional product range but is potentially the most rewarding in supporting your seminars, workshops and events. In time, you may be asked to speak to other audiences on your subject, purely because you have written a book. Often you will be paid well for speaking, but if not, you can always speak for free in exchange for organisers purchasing bulk copies of your book.

Your book doesn't have to be published either. One option is to bind your document yourself with a spiral binder or even in a ring binder. On the surface, this may sound a bit 'amateurish', but these types of products still sell extremely well after a great seminar. We will see later why delegates will still purchase these items.

Your other option is to self-publish on Amazon via Kindle Direct Publishing. The book you are reading is self-published, with Amazon providing everything an author needs to promote and sell their book. In their own words 'Kindle Direct Publishing is Amazon.com's eBook publishing unit launched in November 2007, concurrently with the first Amazon Kindle device. Amazon launched Kindle Direct Publishing, originally called Digital Text Platform, to be used by authors and publishers, to independently publish their books directly to the Kindle Store.'

I have published several books on Amazon and am still amazed at what a simple process it is. Until I looked into it in detail, I had been under the impression that only 'full length' books were accepted by Amazon, but there are vast numbers of extremely short publications that are available on the platform. One of my books has just 28 pages on its Kindle version, but there are many thousands of books with fewer than twenty pages.

When you create a book for Kindle, you simply upload your text, create a cover using a tool they provide (or upload a cover that you have already created elsewhere), choose your book category, set your price and that's it.

Your book/text needs to be formatted for the Kindle device, but again Amazon makes it easy for you by giving you access to a free tool called Kindle Create where you can get the layout right, choose your font etc.

You can also create your own author page on Amazon which people can follow and be kept up to date on your latest books. You can see mine at www.amazon.co.uk/-/e/B0034PMLQ4

Once Amazon approves your publication (which takes about a day), you are live! But here's the best part – Amazon then asks you if you would like to create a paperback version. The process is much the same, and again as soon as your book is live you can then purchase author copies at just the cost of printing – and it's these that you can sell at the back of your seminar room. Alternatively, give a signed copy away as a bonus/incentive for attending in the first place.

You really can't beat having your own published book with a well-known publisher behind you – but if you are looking for speed, convenience and complete editorial control over your book, then self-publishing on Amazon is a great alternative.

You can find a multitude of videos on the topic of self-publishing and how to make money from it on YouTube.

eBooks

Publishing an eBook on the Kindle as described above is a great way to leverage Amazon's global reach. However, if writing a 'proper' book feels too big a step and far too daunting, then a creating and selling a traditional eBook has many advantages.

Writing an eBook, eLeaflet or eReport is a great alternative and in many cases a lot more profitable. For starters, you don't need to find a publisher, negotiate contracts and so on. You can simply sit down and write about your area of expertise.

The normal rules of targeting still apply in that you do need to do your homework as you can't just write any old nonsense in the hope that someone will buy it.

What is an eBook?

An eBook is an electronic version of something you have written. For example, if you are a financial adviser with an expertise in pensions, you could write anything from one to several hundred pages on the subject, or an interesting aspect of the subject – but preferably including information that people actually want, or think they can't live without.

Can't write a couple of hundred pages? That's fine – up to twenty is easy and I've seen may eBooks with no more than ten pages.

The information is written using your usual word processing software, for example Microsoft Word. You then smarten it up, add some illustrations or pictures if you wish and convert it to PDF (Portable Document Format) file on your computer.

By printing to PDF, you are able to perfectly preserve the look and feel of any document or graphics you created, be they presentations, leaflets, brochures, spreadsheets or photographs.

The electronic file can then be sent to any other computer in the world, where the text and images will retain the exact look and formatting that you created. Within the body of the text, you can even incorporate video, sound and live links to websites.

As I mentioned above, many of the normal rules of book publishing don't apply. For example, your eBook can be of *any* length.

It could be a two-page summary of something you say in your seminar, or perhaps a checklist to which people can refer when they are searching for, say, an expert on pensions. Naturally, your checklist would steer the reader to your own service.

The potential for eBooks which support your seminars is therefore endless and often provides you with the platform to sell information which a traditional publisher might otherwise pass by.

Making Profits from eBooks

The best part is the profits. Given that there are none of the normal costs associated with publishing a book (whether through a publisher or self-published), every eBook you sell will make a big profit.

The important thing is that you only ever need to make *one* PDF copy of your leaflet or book. The PDF file sits in your documents file on your computer or in your autoresponder software and you simply email it to the recipient after they have paid for it.

Customers have a variety of ways that they can request and pay for your eBook:

- They can ask and pay for it at your seminar and you email it to them later that day.

- They can email their request after the seminar and you point them to the payment and download page on your website.

- You can bring a laptop or tablet to your event that is already open at your purchase page, which people can use to purchase there and then, with the eBook being delivered to their email address.

- You could give attendees a QR code either on the screen at the end of the event or on a handout, which when scanned by their phone camera takes them to the purchasing page.

- They can pay for it at your event and you give them the eBook on either a CD or memory stick. This adds a little extra cost to your sale, but an alternative is to create a bundle of eBooks and content on the CD/memory stick and sell it at a higher price.

- You could sell membership of a private online group and include access to your eBook(s) within the group.

- They can purchase it from your website (more on this later).

A quick reminder of the benefits of creating and selling eBooks and eGuides:

- They are highly profitable (though can also be given away as 'tasters' to potential clients).

- They can include multi-media and live links to other resources.

- In addition to desktops, they can be read on any mobile device.

- They can be promoted and purchased in a variety of different ways with delivery being automated with Auto Responders (more on this later).

- They provide instant gratification to the online purchaser.

- They enhance the perception of your knowledge, expertise and credibility.

- You can promote your other products and services within the text of eBooks.

- Pages can be personalised to different clients by editing the original documents before converting to a PDF file.

- There are none of the production costs associated with normal publishing.

- The whole sale process can be automated, and with strong online promotion can literally make money for you while you sleep.

Don't ignore CDs and memory sticks as distribution vehicles, because when selling your eBook at events, attendees will prefer something tangible that they can pick up and hold. And of course, there is no reason why you can't also email the PDF to them in addition to the CD – it doesn't cost you anything after all.

To make the product even more attractive, you can create your own CD covers, again by using a variety of free or inexpensive CD cover software tools online or from your local computer store. Many of these include very professional and ready-made templates you simply customise with your title, name and business contacts details. A great online tool is Canva.

To add the finishing touch, I've seen some seminar hosts adding a fake barcode to their CD and also shrink-wrapping the box. Perception is everything!

Now let's do some maths...

The key point to remember is that once you have written your eBook, eGuide, eTips Booklet or whatever, you only have to make *one* PDF file which is then emailed to purchasers. That PDF costs you nothing to produce and you can sell it for whatever you wish.

Your e-materials can be sold for anything from around £4.99 for something fairly basic, to anything up to £64 for a much more comprehensive eBook, eWhite Paper or Special Report.

Let's imagine that you host a seminar or event with forty attendees, and half of them purchase something you have at the back of the room for £25. That's £500 straight off the bat.

And when you work hard to create products that are highly focused on the needs and problems of your attendees, a fifty percent take up rate is not uncommon, with it often being much higher. And think how much extra profit you will make if you also charge an entry fee!

In addition, if you make your eBooks available on your website and promoted through (say) Facebook advertising, the power of the internet opens up your products to anyone in the world.

Consider also offering versions in different languages to broaden their appeal even further. I am currently having some materials translated into Chinese so that they become more accessible to that market. In short, eBooks are pure profit for you. Email is as good as free, so you are not even paying for delivery. And, unless you put your eBook on CD or a memory stick, you aren't paying for packaging either – because there is none!

Tips Booklets

Long before we had email and the internet, Tips Booklets were the seminar host's back of room product of choice – and incredibly popular and profitable they were too. They look and sound quite old-school, but they are still perfect back of room products to sell at your events.

Tips Booklets do 'what it says on the tin'. They give short, sharp tips that show people how to make effective use of and apply the information delivered in your seminar presentation.

Here are some other advantages of Tips Booklets:

- In addition to supporting your presentation, they promote your other services.

- Easy and inexpensive to produce.

- They are quick easy to read.

- They provide practical pointers on how to use the information that was presented.

- They are perceived as providing added value.

- They can be targeted to different audiences.

- They are often shared and passed between colleagues.

- They can be distributed free or sold for profit as products in their own right.

- Some clients will purchase large quantities for redistribution in their own right.

- They can be designed and produced in-house using any popular desktop publishing program.

- They can be repackaged as eGuides available from your website.

In short, they enhance the perception of you and your company as experts and thus encourage people to purchase your other products and services.

In addition, they have very specific design features:

- They should be able to fit into an inside jacket pocket or standard 11 cm by 22 cm envelope.

- They should have simple design, with very limited use of colours, graphics or photographs.

- The cover should be made of glossy card and bound simply with staples or thread.

- They should have 16 to 24 pages maximum.

Their content is also quite specific:

- The subject matter should be clear, simple and restricted to one area of expertise.

- They should be highly targeted and include very specific tips, facts and help – i.e. no waffle!

- The content should be in plain English, clear, factual and designed so that it can be read quickly.

- They should have plain, straightforward titles that create interest. Many of the most successful Tips Booklets have 'How to…' or 'Secrets of…' titles. You may not feel that these are appropriate to your business, so adapt them accordingly.

But remember, Tips Booklets are not a substitute for your presentation or other marketing efforts. They provide support for your marketing messages and should therefore be designed to attract attention, interest, desire and action in their own right.

Consider using or adapting titles along the following lines:

- *Twenty-five Easy Ways to…*
- *…Tips for…*
- *How to Avoid Pitfalls in…*
- *Seven Steps to…*
- *How to Treble Your Sales of … and…*
- *Twenty-five Secrets of Successful…*
- *Revealed – The Insider's Guide to…*
- *Twenty-five Tips to Increase Your Sales of…*
- *Discover Seven Essential…*
- *Twenty-five Tips for Mastering the Art of…*
- *A Hundred and One Ways to Get More from Your…*

Remember – take your product or service and turn your marketing messages into simple 'how to' steps. Don't assume that it will be *too simple* for even your most sophisticated or clued-up clients or customers.

Content continued:

- Try to ensure that the author is a specific person within your business, rather than the business itself. This creates a greater perception of your expertise and readers can associate better with a real person. Ideally one of the speakers at your event should be the author. Yes, some attendees will want a signed copy…

- Don't put too much on each page – spread it over several pages if necessary to keep it clear.

- Include contact details at the start, end and on the back cover.

- Include a page at the back where people can learn how to purchase bulk copies at a discount.

- Include relevant references to your website within the text.

- Include one page briefly describing your other business activities.

- Consider including a perforated tear-out reply-paid form for requesting additional information.

Marketing your Tips Booklet

Depending on your business, your Tips Booklet can be given away free to support other marketing messages or sold as a product in its own right.

If the former, expect to give away many free copies. They are extremely inexpensive to produce, so this should not be a problem.

- Send a copy of the booklet with a press release to all relevant newspapers, magazines and journalists. Think laterally and consider new or unusual publications where your booklet may have appeal. David and Jacqui Smith of HomeSmiths Limited near Haywards Heath, UK once advertised in a private school's parent magazine.

  The advertisement for their upmarket, bespoke home and office furniture cost them about £10 for a year but reached exactly their target customers. So remember – your booklet crystallises the benefits of your main product or service and may well also have appeal to a different market from your usual clients.

- Refer to your booklets in other marketing materials – such as your newsletter, email newsletter and website.

- If referring to your booklet in your email newsletter, include a link to a special page on your website where people can request a copy.

- Produce a PDF version which can be purchased or downloaded from your website.

- Produce a version on CD that can either be given away or sold. Again – include links to further information and other products and services available at your website.

- Include Tips Booklets when making business pitches and proposals.

- Produce a series of booklets and send a copy of just one to existing clients – thus encouraging them to buy more.

- Although your Tips Booklets are inexpensive to produce, they provide real value. Treat them as such and do not give them away like confetti.

- Within your booklet, include a reference to your email newsletter. Encourage readers of your booklet to sign up for the newsletter, which in turn drives them to your website where they can purchase other products or find information.

Pricing your Tips Booklet

If you are going to sell your booklets, remember some simple rules:

- The best sales will be immediately after a presentation or seminar. That means *immediately* after – not after the lunch break or by post the next day.

- Have enough available for everyone in the audience to be able to buy one. Have a box full of spares available in case someone wants to make a bulk purchase there and then.

- Offer discounts for bulk purchases.

- Keep the price simple for 'back of room' sales. Never £X.99 or $Y.95. Stick to round numbers such as £5, £10, $15 and $20 for those paying by cash. This is loose change for many businesspeople.

- Give people the option of paying by credit or debit card.

- If selling your booklet on your website, add postage and packaging. Again, offer discounts for bulk purchases.

- Alternatively, consider giving the booklet away for free on your website, but ask purchasers to cover the cost of postage/shipping.

- Both on and off your website, offer customisation (at increased cost) of the booklet.

Do it now! Try this exercise:

1. What is your main service right now?

2. What are the key benefits of your service?

3. Who are your clients/customers?

4. Who else could be clients/customers?

Now write down ten tips related to your current service that could educate and benefit your clients:

1.

2.

3.

4.

5.

6.

7.

8.

9.

10.

These ten tips will form the basis of your booklet for existing and new clients. Now write again in plain English and then choose a title that shouts benefits!

Some more examples:

- *Ten Ways to Save Tax This Year*
- *Twenty Top Tips to Help You Sell More...*
- *The Insider's Guide to Starting Your Own ... Business*
- *The Complete Guide to Investing in Stocks and Shares*

In summary, use Tips Booklets to:

- Support your presentation and seminar messages
- Establish an image of expertise
- Promote your product or service
- Explore new marketing opportunities
- Distribute added value
- Generate additional income
- Gain free promotion in the press.

Mini-Books

We talked about Tips Booklets earlier, which are at the very low end of the market – really simple, thin pocket-sized guides which fit easily in a pocket or handbag.

Although they may be at the low end of the market, they are still perceived to be valuable and have sold well over many years.

Now let's take it up a notch or two and create something which is still a book containing tips, but which is presented more professionally.

Mini-Books are just that – physically small compared to a traditional paperback and no larger than around 17cms by 12cms. They will typically have fifty to ninety pages, but will have good, if not high production values and therefore something to be proud of.

Examples of these are the 'Authority Guide' series which cover everything from Mindfulness, Conflict Resolution and Financial Forecasting through to Public Speaking, PR for Small Businesses, Performance Management and more.

From the financial advice world, Michelle Hoskin's *Best Practice Makes Perfect* is a great example, and in 86 pages contains 171 tips for advisers. Michelle has also co-authored a second mini book called *The Little Book of Woww!*

Mini-Books can be either published or self-published, the latter being the case for both Michelle's books. If going down the self-published route, yes, it's quick and easy to get your product out there, but if you want it to sell, make sure that you have a market for it.

Case Study Books

Regardless of whether you go down the published, self-published or eBook route, one idea that you could try is the Case Study Book.

Also known as Example Books, these are remarkably easy, and often quick to put together. And if they focus on an area of specialism or particular skill, you can charge a lot of money for them.

Quite simply you put together case studies of 'real' client examples, with one case study per chapter. Clearly, you're not going to identify the real clients behind the examples, though permission from the clients concerned would certainly add an extra layer of credibility.

You can make each case study as long or as short as you wish, and even if you managed just six one-page case studies, you will still have created something of real value that you can either give away as a PDF lead magnet on your website, or indeed package up into something more fancy.

Case study books are perfect for financial advisers – and so easy to put together! One option is to include a range of different case studies as a way to highlight the breadth of the advice or financial planning you do, or a better option is to focus on a particular type of planning that you offer. For example, case studies that focus on:

- A specific age group.

- A specific occupation or niche (e.g. financial planning for doctors).

- A specific group of people (e.g. executives nearing retirement).

- A specific financial planning issue.

- How you have used financial planning tools and software – such as cashflow modelling.

Whichever approach you take, it's important that your case studies are real, because 'made up' examples rarely have the same impact.

A technique used by some of the best seminar hosts in Financial Services is to use real case studies as part of their presentation. I've seen a lot of financial advisers' seminars over the years, and the real case studies always seem to have much more credibility than the contrived ones.

The very best presentations I have seen at financial advice seminars are when they use a *live* case study – where the client concerned is in the room.

In addition to case studies, what other data, reports or presentations have you already created (or could create quickly) that you could compile into a book? Do you have before/after testimonials, swipe files, advertisements, PR examples, email newsletters, articles or blogs?

Maybe you have a specific business skill that has helped you to grow your financial advice business over the years. Perhaps you have been particularly successful with podcasts or working with professional connections and introducers. Gather examples together and compile them into a book. Be sure to put a strong hook in the title to attract your audience.

Take a moment to think over your career as a financial adviser – think about clients, situations and people that you have worked with. What case studies can you come up with which could be included in your own product that can be sold at the back of the seminar room?

Special Reports and White Papers

Another form of writing which can be published or self-published is the Special Report or White Paper. That said, they can also be downloadable PDF files.

Special Reports and White Papers tend to be A4 sized documents which are much more detailed and academic in tone and which address a specific problem or issue.

They can also be education pieces which highlight a new development or perspective on a topic.

Often, they will be high quality, factual and authoritative analysis of research into a topic and can therefore command high prices – often into the thousands of pounds.

For example pensions, investments and retirement planning can be complex, and whilst the financial advice profession is working hard to make it clear and attractive to people, there is very much a place for more in-depth information, and these topics are very well suited to the Special Report or White Paper market.

Perhaps you specialise in employee benefits – it is likely that there will be local companies who would find your writing of value and be willing to pay for your research, analysis and expertise.

Regular publication of White Papers or Special Reports is a great way to differentiate you from others in your industry or profession, and as a result can be valuable in enhancing brand image and awareness.

Typically, you would sell your report on your website or a dedicated page but could just as easily be sold at the back of the room after your seminar or through advertising in HR or other specialist publications.

In addition to the profits that selling your reports can create, 'White Paper Marketing' is a powerful strategy in its own right. Yes, it can be time-consuming, but exponents often remark on the high quality of leads that they can generate.

An important side benefit of writing Special Reports and White Papers is that they can often lead to lucrative consultancy work.

Audiotapes, CDs, Video and DVD videos

It is important to stress again that it is the content of your seminar that delegates have come to hear. Based on this and the quality of your presentation, individuals will make various assumptions about you and your business and will do one of the following:

- Walk away, dissatisfied.

- Walk away satisfied and informed, but with no intention of purchasing your product or service for a variety of reasons.

- Want more information with a view to possibly purchasing your product or service at a later date.

- Want to make an immediate purchase.

It is important to capture those in the second and third groups by making available additional materials and in a different format. Never make assumptions about how people wish to receive their information, so although you are using one main medium to get over your message at your seminar (a 'stand up' presentation), make other communication media available, even if they have to pay for it.

Audio files, CDs, videos and DVDs videos fill this role very well and I would urge you to record some of your material for resale either immediately afterwards, by mail order or from your website. We will show you how to do this shortly.

Other People's Products

If you are an expert on your subject and looking for ways to increase the revenue from your seminars, I have shown above a number of ways that you can substantially increase the total profits from your event, primarily using and repackaging your own expertise.

There is also no reason whatsoever why you cannot sell other people's expertise in the form of their books and audio materials.

Make contact with another businessperson or expert in the same or similar field and offer to promote their products or events for them. It will be unusual for them say no and if anything, they will be flattered and delighted.

Negotiate a commission for selling their tickets, and in return, ask them if they would promote your events. This way, everyone wins!

Membership Sites and Communities

A natural follow on or next step for people to take after attending your events, is to want to 'follow you' and your content.

With the advent of social media 'following' someone has taken on a new meaning. Yes, they can simply click a Follow button on a social networking platform, but some people will want to go a step further, and an increasingly popular way to do this is through private groups and communities where they can get closer access to you.

When you think about it, if someone has found your seminar, workshop or event of value, yes they will want to purchase a product, but they may well be intrigued to find out even more, so joining an online group or community that you run could be ideal – particularly if other people like them are also members.

Depending on the functionality available, having your own private online group gives you many options to further add value to people – or indeed to sell products and services. For example, hosting a course inside an online group or membership site is a simple and popular option, largely because the available software for creating online communities often includes built-in features to host modular courses – ClickFunnels and Mighty Networks being good examples.

A quick Google search will help you find others, and bear in mind that Facebook and LinkedIn groups are also a good basic model you could use to build your community. Indeed, many Facebook and LinkedIn groups have tens of thousands of members and have formed the basis for building very robust businesses around a chargeable membership model.

The chargeable membership model is a powerful and proven business idea, helping you to have that all-important recurring revenue stream.

To learn more on this I highly recommend the excellent book *The Automatic Customer* by John Warrillow. See https://amzn.to/2KJGpkY

There are also membership communities for people who run membership communities! Again, Mighty Networks has a group called Mighty Hosts, whilst there are others such as TRIBE and The Membership Guys. They all provide excellent information on building your online community, including the pros, cons and best practice on charging for membership.

Whilst I've spoken a lot about the importance of writing your own book, I'm increasingly of the view that speakers, consultants, business owners – *anyone* who could sell information – should have their own membership community. And there are distinct benefits of doing so:

- Build community around you, your brand and expertise.

- Communicate instantly with potentially thousands of people.

- People will join who won't necessarily become one-to-one clients, but who will purchase your information products and services.

- Members become advocates and will refer you. Many will become 'raving fans'.

- Listen to what your members are interested in and serve them accordingly.

- A more reliable, stable income stream.

- High potential for upsells and additional profits.

- Your content positions you as an expert, if not *the* expert on a particular topic.

- Membership growth can be exponential with no additional overheads or costs to you.

- It need not be location dependent, but can still offer local 'real' events.

A private membership has in itself, perceived value, because being part of a group of likeminded people is a core benefit of membership communities, particularly when you have a common goal.

People also aspire to be part of such communities, as they have the effect of elevating status – again, particularly when there is a learning goal attached.

I currently run three online membership communities, with two others in the pipeline:

1. **LifeTalk** for IFAs and financial advisers, with groups on Facebook, LinkedIn and Mighty Networks

2. **SpeakerCom** for professional speakers, coaches and consultants on LinkedIn and Mighty Networks

3. **LinkedIn Marketing Secrets** – for anyone who wants better and faster results using LinkedIn in their work or business.

My SpeakerCom group on LinkedIn currently has over 25,000 members but I am in the process of moving the group over to Mighty Networks because the functionality for community development is so much better than on LinkedIn.

LinkedIn Marketing Secrets started life as a Facebook group, but again I am moving it over to Mighty Networks and will then close/archive the Facebook group.

Whilst Facebook and LinkedIn groups are free to run and which can grow very large in a short period of time, there are some serious shortcomings worth keeping in mind:

- The content you see on LinkedIn and Facebook is controlled by algorithms – even in groups. This essentially means that the algorithm tells your members what to see and they often miss the content that you actually want them to see.

- Facebook may be fun, but it is far from conducive to focused networking and there are multiple distractions.

- Facebook actively promotes competitors' groups to your members.

- Both LinkedIn and Facebook are predominantly advertising platforms, which distract from the content in groups. It's also inevitable that Facebook will begin running ads within groups at some point.

Add to that concerns about privacy, data breaches, hate speech, conflict, misinformation, politics etc., I for one would rather use a platform such as Mighty Networks which is both advertisement and algorithm free and has a much more professional feel. They are also specifically designed so that hosts can charge for membership, private groups and courses.

Whilst one of the main benefits of having a membership site is the ability to have potentially thousands of members - size, of course, isn't everything.

Yes, the ability to promote and sell information products to thousands of people is exciting, but a small and high-quality network can be just as valuable and gives you the host, the opportunity to give far greater attention to individual members, particularly those who have joined as a result of attending your seminar or event.

Many membership sites are built round very tight niches, so value is much more important than size. Take these examples of the power of niche communities:

- The Brothers Brick – a community for leading LEGO builders.

    Andrew Becraft founded The Brothers Brick in 2006 to spotlight awesome builds and techniques as well as interview the leading lights of LEGO building. The site now boasts a thriving community of over 300,000 on Facebook.

- Goats of Anarchy – a community for people who care for goats with special needs.

- Young Chefs Academy – courses helping kids build both their skills and their palate.

- Girls Auto Clinic – helping women to get comfortable repairing and caring for their vehicles.

- The Car Seat Lady – videos, guides and installation lessons for growing young families.

- The Sourdough School – help, courses and recipes for baking sourdough.

- Compton Cowboys – men from the inner city who ride through the streets of LA on rescued horses acting as role models for kids.

- The Minimalists – helping people pare down their possessions, and live a healthier more intentional lifestyle.

And four for financial advisers:

The Financial Diet

In their own words: "It's really hard to talk about money. Chelsea Fagin does it for you on her website and 595,000-subscriber YouTube channel. Her tag line is "the luxury of spending less," and she's found massive success helping people save more money and enjoy the things they do buy."

Curtis "Wall Street" Carroll - Self-Taught Financial Redemption

"Behind bars in San Quentin serving a 54-to-life sentence, Curtis Carroll knew he had to turn his life around. So he taught himself to read and then started a financial literacy program for other inmates. His 2017 TED talk, "How I Learned to Read – And Trade Stocks – In Prison" has been viewed over four million times."

The Retirement Answer Man - Relatable Financial Podcast

"We all dream about the moment we can step away from the workforce and into retirement, but Roger Whitney knows not everybody is financially ready. His breezy, engaging podcast has attracted a big listener base of people preparing to quit their day jobs without having to worry about what comes next."

Whatever your community or niche, the communication and content delivery mechanism is almost irrelevant – it's the community that counts, whether it's based round Instagram, YouTube, a Facebook group, Podcast or a dedicated membership site.

Either way, your membership site/community is another fantastic addition to your Value Ladder, and I would highly recommend you consider building one. You can make it chargeable or keep it free but use it as either a high value lead magnet for your other products and services, or as an income stream in its own right.

Look after your Community

However, please don't underestimate how important it is to keep your members engaged – because when you crack this, you have something incredibly valuable for you and your community.

If you are thinking of getting started with your own community, here are some tips to keep in mind:

Firstly, I highly recommend that you join any community which supports community builders, because invariably you will discover a wealth of valuable expertise, tips and help based on practical experiences.

As mentioned earlier, Mighty Hosts is excellent at https://hosts.mn.co

Second, don't stress or give up if you are adding content to your group but hardly anyone is joining. Keep at it – the people will come!

Third, ensure your group or community has an overall theme and goal. Professional community builders call this your *Big Purpose* – your motivation and challenge for your group. It's a phrase coined by Mighty Networks founder Gina Bianchini.

The best Big Purposes for online communities are:

- Specific - You can picture clearly the end state and how each of us in the group will be better for taking on your particular 'quest' or joining your movement.

- Exciting - It's going to be fun and challenging every step of the way.

- Easier Achieved Together - It won't be easy, but if we work together, it's possible.

You can see straight away that online communities work best when members are encouraged to share stories and experiences that everyone else can benefit from. They are less about giving people advice, and more about sharing how people have tackled issues and moved forward.

Within our LifeTalk groups for financial advisers on Facebook and LinkedIn, it's clear to see that the best and most engaging content is when members are first and foremost sharing their stories and experiences. The proof of how valuable this is, is the amazing number of financial advisers who have written to me over the years saying that they have made major business decisions based on the *stories and experiences* of others within the group.

As the group host, what's noticeable is that as soon as a thread tips over into giving advice to one another on a particular course of action, the conversation starts to slow down and often hits a dead end.

One of the characteristics of social media is that people are incredibly quick to share advice, and all too often that becomes overwhelming when dozens or more people pitch into a topic with their advice too.

It's great that people are willing to share advice, but as a community host it's important to set the scene when people join, that what members value more is your experiences. They can then draw their own conclusions and make their own decisions as to what course of action to take on a particular issue they are facing.

By way of an example, this is the Big Purpose we have written for our online community for professional speakers:

> *Within SpeakerCom, we're defining together what it takes to be a great speaker; to build an exciting, profitable and compelling speaking business and to attract more of the speaking opportunities that we really want in 2019.*
>
> *Within the SpeakerCom community, our goal is for every member to gain confidence and make progress towards achieving their speaking goals – through sharing of stories, best practice, failures and successes in a safe and friendly environment.*
>
> *No ads, no algorithms, no negativity or distractions – just support, encouragement, community – and fun!*

Take a moment now to think how you could adapt the Big Purpose above for your own business and online community.

Your online community could fulfil several roles:

- As an added value follow on from your seminars and events
- As a source of prospects to attend future events
- As a vehicle to interact and engage regularly with professional introducers
- As your private 'inner circle'
- As a platform for sharing online courses

Be creative as to how you use your community, but my advice is not to over think it, and to get started straight away by inviting your existing clients to join. Don't obsess about the direction you will take it, but highlight your Big Purpose to your members and over time they will give you clues as to what content will make it valuable for them.

Other tactics to employ in your community include:

- Icebreaker questions – the first thing people see when they join. E.g. *"What do you hope to get from a community of your peers?"*

- Member interviews and stories

- Polls and surveys

- Occasional provocative questions – and I stress *occasional*!

- Monthly themes with relevant weekly content

- Goals for the week

- Share challenges you might have

- 'Wednesday Wins'

- Content organised within topics

- Online and 'real' events

- Weekly summary of the most engaging content over the previous seven days

Regardless of the topic or theme of your online community, there are also lots of fun things you can do to engage members which always go down well, such as:

- On Fridays ask members to tell you about their week in Just Three Words

- Post a picture taken during the week

- Post a picture of your pet

- Describe what you're best at in two words

- Tech Tuesdays – favourite apps and software

- What is your favourite album of all time?

- Fuck Up Fridays! Tell us about something that has gone wrong this week.

  Yes, I have seen this one being used, and despite the language, it always gets a good response. Depending on who you are targeting with your community, clearly this one is optional!

You might think that asking people to post a picture of their pet in a professional forum is a bit trivial. But as part of your overall content strategy, occasional use of posts like this work very well. Often you will see huge numbers of your members taking part.

Questions are a great way to engage your community. I have seen all of these used to good effect:

- Where did your talents come from – luck, hard work or your genes?

- Which person outside of your family has had the most influence on your life?

- What is a project you are planning, but just can't get started?

- What was the career you never had?

- Which personal development books have really changed you?

- What are your favourite podcasts?

- What is one thing you want to improve this week?

- How would you describe your brand?

- What are you currently procrastinating about in your business?

- What do you want to be held accountable for this week?

I have dozens more questions like this – please drop me a line for a list if you would find it useful.

I'd love you to join either **LinkedIn Marketing Secrets** or **SpeakerCom** and be part of *my* community. You can find them at https://linkedin-marketing-secrets.mn.co and https://speaking-professionals.mn.co/

And there's also **LifeTalk** for financial advisers at www.facebook.com/groups/AdviserLifeTalk

If nothing else, take a look at the landing pages to see how they have been set out and presented to potential members.

Miscellaneous Sales

Other than your repackaged business expertise, it is perfectly reasonable to sell a number of more frivolous items such as tee-shirts, hats, mugs, pens, mouse mats, golf balls, playing cards etc. It should go without saying that everything you sell should at least have your website address on it.

Always try to have some miscellaneous items available, as you will be surprised what attendees at your seminar will buy, particularly if the event has gone well. If you have put on an excellent seminar or workshop, your coasters, mouse mats and pens fulfil the desire to take something home – the souvenir mentality that always kicks in when we have enjoyed something. Don't give away your items at the back of the room, as the souvenir becomes more valuable to them if they paid for it.

Additional points about Creating and Selling Products

Do remember the normal rules about presenting items for sale. Even if they are at the back of the room there are a few things you can do to increase the perception of their value:

- Accept credit cards.

- Price your products at round numbers so that you minimise the amount of time trying to find change when people pay by cash.

- If you have a 'stampede' to your back of room table, you will need helpers unless you can get through sales quickly. I always recommend that you have at least one helper, as many people who make a purchase also want to talk to you – sometimes for long periods of time. You must spend time with them if that's what they want.

- During your seminar, give away a copy of your book or CD as the prize in an easy competition.

    Ideally, give the prize to someone seated near the back of the room and ask people in the audience to pass it back to the winner. This way, some of the audience get to *touch* the product and glance quickly at the cover and this creates a strong desire to own the item themselves.

- Try to obtain third party endorsements for your products and print it either on the packaging or on a board that is visible by the products.

- Offer customisation of your products for bulk purchases.

- Offer discounts for bulk purchases.

- With every product you sell, include a simple leaflet detailing other back of room products that you sell, plus of course details of your main product or service and website address.

- Think carefully about where you place the table displaying your products. They are called 'back of room' products because they are generally sold 'at the back of the room'. But modern venues at hotels and conference centres aim to make best use of space and you may find it impractical to have your table at the back of the room.

  At the very least, you want your products to be somewhere that the delegates will walk past – preferably when they are on their way in and out of the room.

  Someone once told me that the ideal place is in the corridor immediately outside the hall you are in – between coffee and the bathrooms! You will find that even a few inches in the wrong place can kill sales.

I once had a table at the front of a lecture theatre right next to the door, so that everyone could see my CDs etc. on the way in, at the break and then again at the end. The only problem was that the table had been placed on the stage I was presenting from, a step up of about 50 centimetres. Whilst I sold about 15 CDs, the step was too high for many to be bothered to climb.

Finally, offer commission to people for selling your products – be they your main product or your back of room materials. You often find that if you put on a really good seminar, there will be somebody present who is so taken by your message, your enthusiasm and your products that they will be happy to promote and sell them themselves!

How to Create Information-Based Products – Quickly

Not everyone will find that they have the time or ability to create written products, whether a 'proper' book or an eBook. They may also feel that they cannot afford to hire a crew to record and produce a professional video.

However, there are a number of alternatives which can help you to quickly produce high quality additional products to boost the overall profits of your seminar. Most people should find there is at least one method suits them. Here are some ideas for you.

Method 1

As we have discovered, an eBook can be of any length. The word 'book' can be little misleading unless you really are going to produce a work of significant length and value which has been designed specifically for e-marketing.

However, it is possible to produce information-based electronic products with relative ease, which can be sold both at and after your seminars.

First, consider carefully exactly what is your main area of expertise. If you are satisfied that you really are an expert on the subject, write down if you have a particular speciality in the subject or are offering something unique.

Follow this simple model to create your book and you'll be surprised how quickly it will come together:

First, write the back cover for the book. Yes, start at the end, as writing the back cover first gives you amazing focus on what you are going to cover. Grab a couple of books off your bookshelf and copy the style and approach. Some are written in bullet points whilst others have a few paragraphs that highlight the benefits the reader will get.

Next, write a comprehensive overview of your topic. This can be anything from two to ten pages.

Then, decide on twenty main points that you intend to make and then between two to four sub-points for each main point. Then write two pages on each of your sub-points. Before you know it, you will have written about 200 pages.

Make sure it is proofread, checked for grammar and spelling and given a title along the lines of those described earlier (e.g. *How To…, Twenty Ways to…* and so on). You may also wish to include some artwork such as photographs, graphics and diagrams, but avoid using lots of different pieces of clip art as this can cheapen the look of your publication.

When you are happy that your text is as good as you can make it, print it straight from your word processing software as a PDF file. Done – you've created a digital product. And as mentioned earlier you could also publish it for the Kindle on Amazon.

Again, please do not obsess about perfection. Thousands of books each year never see the light of day because their authors couldn't get their manuscripts finished. This week I was speaking with the Head of Creative Writing at a leading university, and she told me that not being able to finish a book, story or manuscript is very common amongst students, so they 'force' students to finish each piece of work before moving on to something else.

I also know of at least two business books, each with two hundred pages and each written in one day. Yes, there are some grammatical errors here and there, but these became global best-sellers regardless of occasional lack of polish.

Finally, create an audio version of your text and, you've guessed it – sell that too.

Method 2

The second method essentially reverses Method 1.

Use your mobile phone or a separate microphone to record you speaking or giving a presentation – a seminar ideally.

Then transcribe the recording – either manually yourself or using the services of a transcriber found on Fiverr.com or similar outsourcing site.

My current favourite is to use Rev.com where for (currently) $1 per minute you can have your audio or video file transcribed. Voice recognition services are also available, but Rev uses real transcribers and the service is excellent.

So much so, that it is worth getting into the habit of recording every presentation, speech or seminar that you give, so that they can be transcribed for you – thus building up a bank of written content that you can turn into products.

If you don't want to transcribe the audio soundtrack at all, you can use your digital recording as just that – an audio recording. If you want to copy it straight to CD or memory stick 'warts and all' that's fine. People will still buy it after your seminars if the content is good.

Another interesting way to produce an e-leaflet, e-brochure or eBook is to recognise that what you are producing is not actually a book in the true sense of the word. And as such it is fun to try different ideas to format the text.

One suggestion is to record a colleague or friend interviewing you on your subject. The interview would then be transcribed using Rev.com or similar.

To give the interview additional credibility, try to find an interviewer who is also very knowledgeable on your subject. Whilst the questions can be scripted in advance, an interviewer who knows about the subject is likely to be more spontaneous in their questioning.

When you create your final product, make it clear right from the outset that this product was created from a live interview, so it will read much more informally than a traditional book.

And yes, you could also sell audio copies of the interview itself.

Method 3

Finally, if possible I would strongly recommend that you film one of your seminars or workshops, or even hire a small studio. The former is preferable as the film also shows the audience and their (hopefully) positive reactions to your talk.

Once edited and packaged you will have a 'live performance' that can be sold either at the back of the room at future seminars, on your website or by mail order.

This option is the most expensive option, but potentially extremely lucrative. Today there are many small film production companies in what is a very competitive marketplace. Ask to see examples of their work and then negotiate strongly.

Make sure your quote includes editing and try to attend the editing session, as you and your material must be shown in the best possible light.

Wherever possible, try to have at least two cameras and opt for the best quality format that you can afford.

Some production companies will give you a small number of free copies of the final edit, but try to negotiate as many as you can, as duplication of your film will cost extra.

That said, you can also film it yourself. You really don't need to have Steven Spielberg production values, because what people really want is the content – particularly if they are making their purchase immediately after your seminar. It is important however, that your sound is clear. Again, it's easy to find inexpensive microphones online.

As far back as 2005, financial advisers Taylor and Taylor Financial Services of Bolton in the north of England were recording their own seminars and selling them as DVDs to future event attendees. And this was before recording video on mobile phones was commonplace, so think how easy it is to do today!

Why will People buy these Products?

In addition to souvenir type products, we can see that it is relatively easy to produce a number of information-based products which you can sell immediately after your seminar or workshop, by mail order or from your website.

But will anyone want to buy them, particularly if they have been produced in the office or at home? Surely people only want top quality these days and will not buy something unless they have high production values?

It may surprise you to learn that many of the best sales and personal development tapes available for the last forty years were either recorded live in front of an audience or in the speaker's study or back bedroom. Many were recorded using portable mono cassette recorders and extremely cheap microphones.

Today we have the benefit of digital technology, which can produce broadcast quality recordings. Even our home video equipment can now produce extremely high-quality pictures when used correctly.

The point though is not the quality of the recordings or the packaging (though don't *underestimate* its importance), it is the quality of the content and material that counts. I cannot stress this enough because it is the key to making big supplementary profits from your seminars.

Whether you sell a video on flower arranging or a Tips Booklet on interior design, it is the quality of the content that will make the difference between your seminars just paying for themselves (if at all) or generating significant additional income in their own right.

So now your total income looks like this:

Total income (TI) = ticket sales income (TSI) + main product/service sales income (PSI) + referral income (RI) + additional product income (API) + consulting income (CI)

Exercise

Consider the business you are in, whether a financial adviser, vet, accountant, interior designer, furniture manufacturer, artist, marketing consultant, IT consultant, trainer, florist, gardener, hairdresser, professional golfer, masseur, library agent, photographer, the list is endless.

Write down three aspects of your work that could form the basis of a seminar. Think specifically what expertise you could demonstrate or highlight and the benefits that would bring people:

1.

2.

3.

Now, write down three information-based e-products that you could either sell or give away at or after your seminar:

1.

2.

3.

Write down some objectives for you for hosting your own seminar:

1.

2.

3.

And finally, write down some objectives you want to set for your attendees – what is that you want them to act on or do as a result of attending your event:

1.

2.

3.

Congratulations – you've now got the basis of your plan written down and you can start moving forward.

Summary

In Part 1 we have examined:

- The reasons why seminars should become a key marketing strategy for all financial advisers

- How to plan your events

- How to get people to turn up

- How to turn your seminars into high profit money-making events

In Part 2 we will look at how to present your messages with power, impact, clarity, confidence and conviction – because if you can't, do not expect the audience to want to talk to you afterwards about your products or services.

You absolutely *must* be able to present your expertise effectively so that you inspire, entertain and inform the audience. If you can do that, they will be your friends for life – and loyal advocates for your business.

Part 2

Getting Your Business Message Across with Impact, Power and Authority

Presentation is Everything

Presentation *(n)*. 1. The act of presenting or state of being presented. 2. The organisation of visual details to create an overall impression. 3. A verbal report presented with illustrative material, such as slides, graphs, etc.

Spin *(vb)*. To present news or information in a way that creates a favourable impression.

To the horror of parents of teenage children everywhere, we live in a world which is dominated by image. Popstars, footballers and social media pages shout at our offspring to tell them what latest gear they must be seen in if they are to be considered cool, chic and trendy. Never mind your personal skills – if you *look* good, that tells your friends everything they need to know about you...

In business too, companies are increasingly judged not just on how good their products are, but how they present themselves to the outside world. We're told the importance of effective branding and the need to differentiate ourselves beyond merely price. We hear how branding will build customer loyalty, increase trust and help to build our customer base.

Customers now engage with and purchase from brands based on the perception of how they conduct themselves within the wider world. How they source their raw materials, how they support local communities, their attitude towards diversification and equality, and their impact on the environment. Our brand reputation is everything.

This is equally so on the day of our seminar or workshop – though most of us in small businesses do not yet have an established, recognisable brand image that is known to stand for something of value. In fact one of the main purposes of putting on the seminar is to start building a brand, because seminars and workshops can be particularly effective at conveying your company's worth and image in the marketplace – particularly at a local level.

If nothing else, hosting a seminar differentiates you from other financial advisers.

Financial planner and adviser coach Michael Kitces in the USA often talks about a *"crisis of differentiation"* amongst advisers, and he is correct.

Online it is extremely difficult to differentiate one adviser from another because their websites all say the same thing, they use the same pictorial themes and the words and phrases used to describe their services and values are remarkably similar.

I can do a party-piece at conferences where I can write the About Us page for just about any financial advice firm in the UK – without having met them. What's more they will be really pleased with the result.

I guarantee you that advisers who host seminars and client events have no difficulty differentiating themselves and are perceived as having much more credibility and expertise.

In reality, they may have no more credibility and expertise than the next IFA firm, but they will be perceived to be more professional and have greater authority in their locale.

Presenting an Image

But are you actually portraying the image you want people to see? How many times have you been to a party or social event where there are strangers present about whom you form an instant opinion – and very often *before* you have even spoken to them?

Instantly and subconsciously we make assumptions and come to conclusions on everything from their politics to their trustworthiness. We do it automatically, without thinking. And very often, just as we are often correct in our assumptions, isn't it the case that we are often *entirely wrong*? But by then it can be too late – because first impressions count. Perception is reality.

If it is possible to build an apparently detailed impression of someone across a dinner table who we have never met, just imagine our response to someone standing in front of us who is making a presentation. Particularly someone who, however well they disguise it, is ultimately trying to sell us something! Our senses literally go into overdrive as we analyse every sound, movement and gesture and it's not very long at all before we reach conclusion, 'I don't like him', or 'I don't trust her'.

Some say it only takes fifteen seconds for us to complete the analysis process – I don't know, it may be thirty seconds or even as long as twenty minutes, but at the end of the day it doesn't matter. You don't get a second chance to make that first impression.

Why then is this simple point so often ignored by presenters and what can we do about it? If I had a pound for every time I've seen someone start a presentation by saying *"Sorry, the font on the slides is a bit small..."* or *"Sorry I'm not used to presenting..."* or *"Sorry, I haven't had much time to rehearse this..."*

Please don't be sorry. Instead, do something about it, because you have made a poor impression on your audience before you've even got started.

Unfortunately many businesses are more concerned about how many Likes their latest tweet got on Twitter than working on the skills needed to make effective, authoritative and compelling presentations. Many *believe* that delivering strong presentations is important to achieving business success, but don't exactly go out of their way to ensure that they have the skills to give their best performance.

I can't stress how important this is, because being able to speak and present at seminars, workshops and live events is one of the most effective sales and marketing tools at your disposal.

The good news is that you can learn all the skills you need – regardless of whether or not you enjoy public speaking.

Presentation Skills

Just look at the CVs of many businesspeople, and you'll find under the 'Training and Courses' section 'Presentation Skills' popping up once every five to ten years or so.

For many, there is no real technical meat to absorb on such courses and they are often seen as a bit of a skive. Presentation skills courses aren't that difficult to get out of either if you have something else to do. *"I've been talking to groups of people for 25 years, so I think I know how to make a presentation"* is a common excuse amongst senior executives.

Or is the problem something else? Like the fact that delegates on these courses are usually filmed giving role play presentations? Good old fear has a big part to play.

In short, presentation skills training is not everyone's idea of fun. Whilst it is intended to help you, it can in fact be extremely stressful. In his excellent book *And Death Came Third*, Business networking expert Andy Lopata quotes a New York Times survey from 1984 where people were asked what they fear most. Death came third on the list, with walking into a room full of strangers and public speaking coming first and second.

But this is no excuse.

Let's get this said straightaway. No matter how good your expertise, credibility and content, your presentation is everything. Like it or not, it tells people everything about you, your business, your service, your trustworthiness and your expertise. Your presentation skills are the oil which aids the smooth communication of your expertise. And even though the act of standing and talking to the group elevates your position of authority, this image will crash down around you if you are unable to present your messages with clarity, confidence and conviction.

So, it follows that if one of the objectives of your seminar is to raise the awareness of your business and its expertise, it is vital that you possess the necessary skills to make it happen. Few are born with the skills to present effectively, just as there are no 'born chefs' or 'born accountants' or 'born footballers'. Yes, we possess certain attributes which help, but it takes hard work, commitment and practice to become really good.

Unlike a lot of material on presentation skills, I'm not going to look in any depth at the usual issues – like the importance of not jangling change or keys in your pocket – that's all a bit old school. What I am including though are my own observations over 40 years of making and being on the receiving end of many thousands of presentations.

When I ask people what is most important to them when listening to a speaker, the results often prove less predictable than I would have imagined:

- 43% say that the speaker should motivate them to take action

- 28% say the speaker should be passionate about their subject

- 16% say that the presentation should be simple and easy to understand

- 13% say that the presentation should be relevant to their needs

- 0% say the presentation must include visual aids

I could write another book analysing the figures in minute detail, but the results do support my observations of both inexperienced and experience presenters at countless talks over many years. And it is the fact that people want to be 'motivated to take action' rather than to be 'motivated to take notes' which interests me most in the context of Seminar Selling.

The whole purpose of our seminars is to promote our business by highlighting and demonstrating our expertise and if it is the case that people want a presentation to motivate them to take action, then all the better! What we don't want to happen is for people to sit and enjoy the talk and then do nothing. It is for this reason that presentation skills are included in this book, so that we can make absolutely sure that our talk *really does* motivate people to take action.

Confidence

"Believe in yourself! Have faith in your abilities! Without a humble but reasonable confidence in your own powers you cannot be successful or happy."

Norman Vincent Peale, author of *The Power of Positive Thinking*

Hands up who enjoys making presentations?! Not everyone, that's for sure. There are all kinds of statistics which supposedly show that most of us fear making presentations more than death or flying or spiders or whatever.

But despite the growth of social media, sales and marketing presentations are an integral part of everyday business life. Their value in communicating information or motivating people simply can't be ignored and being *competent* at presentations is no longer good enough. Despite the internet and a whole host of communication technology, there is still nothing to beat face-to-face interaction between two human beings.

There's something about 'live' performance which is captivating and inspirational when done well. Nothing can beat the buzz in an audience those few moments just before a live concert gets underway – weather rock, jazz or classical. And our heroes rarely disappoint. But what is it that creates this buzz?

Certainly in an audience there is an air of excitement and expectation which is multiplied many times over by the sheer volume of people present. Perhaps it is because we feel we already have a relationship with the band, soloist or orchestra and we're at the concert to enjoy the company of an old friend? Unless your audience is made up of mainly existing clients who know and love your product or service, you are going to have to work hard to create that same atmosphere and buzz. And if that buzz isn't there, you will have to compensate in other ways – so a key element in your presentation is impact.

What are the factors that determine Impact in a Presentation?

There are many things which come into play here, including your content, your appearance, your delivery and so on. But as we said earlier, from your delegates' perspective, the impact of your seminar actually starts with your first piece of promotional material for the event.

Subconsciously people will start to form an opinion about you and your business as soon as they see the first advertisement or the first leaflet or your website. On the day of the seminar itself, the degree to which you make an impact will be determined by the delegates very early on.

- Are the directions to the venue clear?
- Is it easy to find a parking space?
- Is parking free?
- Is the venue attractive and distinctive?
- Is the seminar room easy to find?
- Is it comfortable?
- But most importantly, are the delegates greeted personally by the seminar host?

This is one of the most important things I can say about seminar presentations. Make life easy for yourself by building a relationship with as many of your delegates as possible before the event gets underway. Be relaxed, friendly and open with people and shake hands with them.

This is another good reason to phone up and thank each person when they make their booking. If you don't already know them, here's your chance to start building the relationship, so that when they turn up at your event, you both feel that you already know each other.

Ask questions about their journey, for example *"Where have you come from today?"* and on no account look as though you are still setting up or looking over your notes. Now is the time for the audience. Quite often, as part of your 'meet and greet' activities you will pick up or overhear snippets of information about people which may be of use in your presentation later.

The relationships you build as people are arriving will start to create a buzz of your own – not quite on the scale of the buzz before a Metallica gig, but getting there! And it's this buzz that will help to create impact for you. Meeting and greeting people in person will also help to build your confidence.

Build Trust

Another useful tip is to make physical contact with every attendee. Clearly there is a need for care here, but what is important is that at the very least you shake hands with them. Some anthropologists believe that the only reason we shake hands when we meet someone, is to prove that we are not concealing a weapon – so in essence this is a trust building activity.

And if someone trusts us, they are more likely to engage with us – which is exactly what we want if we are hosting a seminar or event.

Take their Coats

For many speakers and presenters, ego can be a potential problem – I've even seen seminar hosts waiting 'backstage' while their guests arrive, so they can make an impactful entrance when everyone is seated.

In fact, there are better ways to create an impact – like by being a normal human being. That includes doing normal things like taking people's coats, pouring them coffee and showing them to their seats. Yes, you the seminar host and main presenter should be doing these things (along with your team if you have one), because they oil the wheels of building relationships.

Talking to and engaging with your guests at this early stage also helps to relax you before everything gets started. Just talking to people in the room that you are using helps to warm you up. And it's really important that you do get warmed up…

Can you imagine your country's rugby team not having a warmup before a World Cup match?

Can you imagine a world class concert pianist not having a warmup before taking to the stage at the Royal Albert Hall?

Can you imagine an athlete not having a warmup before running the 1500 metres?

To be perceived as professional, you need to act like a professional. So ideally, you should have a run through of the first five minutes or so of your presentation, but failing that, spend time talking to your guests as they arrive.

Nerves

Nerves affect all of us before a presentation and rightly so. When we feel nerves, it is our body preparing ourselves to do the best job possible.

In fact, it goes back to our fight or flight mechanism, where if we are confronted by a tiger outside our cave, we have two choices – fight or run. Either way, our body needs adrenaline and noradrenaline to be released into the blood stream. The same goes for that moment before a big presentation – our body needs to prepare us to perform at the highest level possible.

To some people it is a very uncomfortable feeling, but on the plus side, nerves help to tame presenters at the other end of the scale, i.e. those supremely confident with ego problems! Either way, when you feel nervous before a presentation, you can reassure yourself that what you are currently experiencing is your body preparing itself to take action.

For most people, nerves actually dissipate after a short while as you get into your stride, particularly if you know your subject inside out and have rehearsed.

There are a variety of techniques for easing nerves and building confidence, but the ones which I favour include:

- Stand up straight and let the oxygen get to your lungs.

- 'Act' confidently and authoritatively. As Professor Lord Robert Winston once said, *"Act authoritatively and you will be perceived as authoritative"*

- Spend at least 15 minutes a day for the week beforehand visualising yourself performing well. See the audience smiling and nodding and agreeing with what you are saying. Imagine how you will feel when they are clapping and then coming up to talk to you afterwards. The human mind can't tell the difference between something that is real and something that is vividly imagined, so use creative visualisation to help your nerves. It won't just help your nerves – in fact it will actually enhance your performance.

- Smile at people and look them in the eye. You know it makes sense!

- Take a brisk walk outside or around the hotel or venue and breathe deeply. This is something I do before every talk I give – whether to five people or five thousand people.

- Rehearse, rehearse, rehearse and rehearse some more. Do not ignore this part. Ideally, your final presentation should be complete some weeks prior to the event to give you more than sufficient time to become completely familiar with it. Give yourself enough time to completely immerse yourself in your material so that you know it inside out and back to front. Believe me, it does wonders for your confidence.

- Have additional material available in reserve with which to answer questions. You should try to anticipate what questions will be asked, so that you can use this material at a moment's notice. This makes you look very confident in the eyes of the audience, particularly if the questions are asked at the end when it looks like you've already said everything. It will also enhance their perception of your expertise.

- Have a 'proper' rehearsal of the first five to ten minutes of your talk – ideally in the seminar room. Like sportspeople, this 'limbers you up' ready for action. If for some reason you can't fit in rehearsal in the seminar room, try reading out loud for fifteen minutes, either at home or in your hotel bedroom.

- Don't drink tea or coffee (or alcohol for that matter). Ideally drink water that is at room temperature.

But above all, the most important thing to remember which will boost your confidence is to focus strongly on the audience and their needs. Just as the key to good salesmanship is to listen and understand the needs of clients, so too should you pay close attention to your seminar audience.

Focus on making your talk valuable and memorable for them, look them in the eye, observe their reactions to what you are saying and pay attention to their body language. If you have done your research and conducted surveys, your content should already be focused on their needs, but back it up in the way you deliver your material. In short, show and demonstrate that you care about them. The switch of focus from yourself and your own concerns to those of your audience makes a remarkable difference in your confidence and consequently in the impact of your delivery.

Finally, we will talk about this again a little later, but if you want to be confident in yourself and your presentation, you absolutely must rehearse over and over again.

Only last night on Strictly Come Dancing, I heard one of the judges Craig Revel Horwood saying to a competitor, that if they wanted to be confident in their dance…

"Repetition, repetition, repetition until it becomes second nature. Once it becomes second nature, then you can add performance."

Clarity

"Your audience will be noticing everything about you, so your visual image should reflect the qualities and values you want to project. You may, for example, wish to convey professionalism, integrity and personal warmth. Make sure your appearance is in keeping with these values.

Remember too that solid blocks of colour in a suit and shirt, rather than a pattern, will always have more impact.

Tip: Find out what your background colour will be, and then try to wear contrasting colours as you want to stand out from, not merge with, what's behind you."

Deborah Hall, Business TV presenter and media trainer

So you've done your research, you've got a room full of delegates and you've made a great initial impact. Now what?

One of the problems with experts who speak is that their passion for their subjects can sometimes be a little overwhelming. Often they have the mistaken belief that their sheer enthusiasm will sweep the audience off their feet. In fact, it may sweep them out of the room if they are not careful.

People are naturally drawn to experts, but it is vital that the passion in their message does not obscure the message in itself. Therefore, clarity of message is extremely important, and this couldn't be more important than for financial advisers, because people attending financial advisers' seminars have, by definition, come for clarity.

Clarity is also important because it aids recall. After all, we do want the audience to actually remember what we are saying and ideally, to act on it.

Here are some ideas to help improve the clarity of your message:

- Stick to the point and avoid going down side roads in your presentation.

    Keep the content relevant to the audience's needs. If you go off at too many tangents, you will simply confuse people. Give them as close as you can to what they are expecting – though keep in mind that there will always be one or two in the audience who will be expecting more than you were planning to give. These people will be the first to ask questions.

- Never assume that everyone knows what you're talking about and *don't use jargon*. Fine between colleagues, but not at a seminar, even if many of the audience have a good understanding of your topic. Use of jargon can also imply arrogance, which is not exactly conducive to building relationships.

- As well as keeping your language so that everyone understands you, keep the overall message clear by only covering one main theme of your presentation e.g. ways to save tax.

Within that one theme, try to make no more than three big points with a couple of examples for each – particularly for shorter events. In this example, you could go on to talk about four main ways to save tax, such as through pension contributions, tax free savings plans, utilising exemptions and transfer of assets between partners.

Remember, don't get too detailed because the name of the game is to motivate people enough to ask you for more information directly related to their personal circumstances. If you get too heavy, you only confuse them and they will only be motivated to leave.

- Rehearse, rehearse, rehearse

    Another reason why rehearsal is so important is that it helps to 'iron out the creases' in the language of your talk.

- Keep quiet!

    Don't be afraid to use silence in your presentation to give people time for the information to sink in, or for them to ask a question. Silence can be very effective as both a tool to give people a breathing space and also to build drama and power in a talk. It can sometimes feel quite disturbing for a speaker to include long passages of silence – even just three to four seconds will feel uncomfortable, but remember, less is more.

- Use repetition

It may sound a bit obvious, but repetition is a great way to clarify your points and there is evidence to show that repeating something several times can increase the chances of it being remembered from around 10% to 90%.

Quite a lot of speakers have trouble with this presentation technique, because they feel they may come over as too authoritative if they say something like *"Let me repeat that…"*. But you don't necessarily have to repeat a sentence verbatim over and over again; with practice you can make the same point many times, but in different ways.

- Move about

    Movement and gestures can help you to emphasise and clarify points. Presenters often worry about what they should do with their hands during a talk, but if you are an expert and passionate about your subject, your hands and arms will (trust me) take on a life of their own. Focus on giving the audience value, not on yourself.

    But be careful when moving about and don't overdo it. Unless you are Tony Robbins, you will find it difficult to get away with running around the stage and fist pumping. Use movement to emphasise points or to start new sections of your talk.

    Also try to avoid repeatedly stepping forward and backwards – a common problem with speakers who don't feel very confident about their content.

    When you rehearse your presentation, either ask a

friend or colleague to look out for this – or film yourself and keep an eye out for bad habits.

- Use humour

    Humour can either be very effective or very dangerous! There are a few rules which need to be stuck to. First, unless you are naturally funny and known for being funny, avoid humour. Second, if you are going to be funny, don't tell jokes. Many presenters believe that a presentation should start with something fairly light and so why not give the audience a joke?

    Yes, as we said earlier, impact is very important, but unless you are a comedian with years of experience telling jokes in front of audiences in smoke filled clubs, just don't do it. You will be no more able to do this well than perform open-heart surgery. Leave jokes to people who are experts in telling jokes.

    As an alternative to using humour, tell stories. Personal stories help people to connect with you at a human level, and an average story will always be better received than a poorly told joke.

    However, you *are* an expert on yourself, so one way of introducing humour it's to say something self-deprecating – about your hair, your height, your weight or whatever. This approach saves us all the embarrassment of a joke that falls flat and shows the audience humility which is a very good trait in a presenter.

And even if you are going to use a little self-deprecating humour, use it sparingly and above all, rehearse it –many, many times over!

Using Different Media

Use different media to support the spoken word. Note 'support'. We will look at use of Microsoft PowerPoint in a moment, but there are a number of other ways you can support your message.

One of the best presentations I have ever seen was by a Swiss gentleman named Rolf Hüppi, who at the time was the worldwide CEO of Zurich Insurance.

On a visit to the UK he addressed the troops for ninety minutes summarising the financial performance of the group over the past year. He spent the entire presentation rooted to the spot, without any use of PowerPoint, flip charts or slides. He spoke with clarity, confidence, authority and conviction.

Then, at the most important part of his presentation (which described his vision for the coming five years) took a black felt pen from an assistant and drew about six lines on an overhead projector acetate. He then turned a handle on the side of the projector, winding a clean piece of acetate onto the illuminated surface.

After drawing six more lines, Mr Hüppi reached his conclusion and left the stage. It was a stunning performance, breaking many of our 'rules' of presenting, but it was the one, brief use of different media which captured everyone's attention. Simple and extremely effective.

I know of a couple of other professional speakers who still use an overhead projector with acetate slides. Without exception it works extremely well – and this is partly because instead of presenting readymade slides, you are creating them by hand, live in front of people.

As we have seen, the good old-fashioned overhead projector can still play its part, as can the humble flipchart. Indeed, I believe that these two presentation tools can actually be better at presenting certain types of information than PowerPoint.

For example, when conveying statistical information, graphs are often the best way of getting your point across. However, there is nothing to beat graphs which are drawn 'live' in front of the audience. And 'live' is the right word because the act of drawing them brings the numbers to life so that they mean more to your delegates. You do need to practice this approach – in particular drawing the elements of the graph in the *right order* so as to maximise the effect.

For other use of flipcharts, remember to:

- Keep them simple
- Have no more than four to five words per line
- Keep to a maximum of five lines on the sheet
- Use big writing, preferably in capitals
- Use blue or black ink and make highlights in red. Never write main points in red or green because they are hard to read at the back of the room

Finally, if you are speaking in a room which is longer than forty feet, check before you start your presentation to see if your writing can be seen by people at or near the back.

Finally, magic and illusion is another good way of supporting your message. It should be used very sparingly (unless you are putting on a magic show) and only as a metaphor for something you are saying.

It must make a point or it will distract from your message, but when used carefully it can be devastatingly effective. I suppose that it should go without saying that its use should always be extremely well rehearsed! If you are interested in exploring this presentation technique, there are a number of business trainers who offer coaching and I would highly recommend John Hotowka as an expert in combining magic with business presentations.

A Few Words on using PowerPoint and other Presentation Software

Remember that the title of this chapter is Clarity. And that is precisely what PowerPoint should be used for. But all too often precisely the opposite occurs.

PowerPoint is now such a magnificent tool that it is easy to get carried away with its fantastic array of functions, leaving the viewer's head spinning in a whirl of colour and animation which the Walt Disney Corporation would be proud of. Whilst the enthusiasm is to be commended, such an audio-visual fantasy does little to help the presenter get his or her message across with clarity.

At the other end of the scale is the user who uses PowerPoint without any of the bells and whistles, but who completely misses the point of using visual aids. As we said earlier, PowerPoint is to *support* your message and can be very effective in doing so.

People at presentations remember more of what they see (30% more) than what they hear (about 10%) and the combination of the two can result in people remembering very much more (50%). But the effect will be completely lost if the presenter uses the software as a crutch for themselves rather than as a tool to enlighten the audience.

Evidence for this is over-cluttered slides where the speaker merely reads the bullet points, overuse of graphs and charts and overuse of clipart. This is just plain laziness and causes audiences to pay more attention to the slides than the speaker. Your presentation is a direct reflection of you and your business and whilst many people *think* that using PowerPoint enhances their image, often the opposite is the case.

As a final word on PowerPoint, I also think that its overuse can create additional unwanted stress on presenters. So much time is put into preparing the slides and animations and worrying whether the technology will work that the speaker inevitably gets distracted from what they are trying to achieve. In other words, the focus stays on themselves and not on the audience where it should be.

Presenting to a group of people can be stressful enough as it is, so don't make things worse by giving yourself extra things to worry about.

Storytelling

In recent years I have become increasingly interested in the power of storytelling in presentations. It is something that good presenters do all the time anyway and often without realising it.

We all like to hear a good story and are naturally drawn to people who tell stories well – whether with friends, in the pub or at the supermarket. But telling stories as part of a business presentation or a seminar also has very practical benefits, not least of which is the way they help to clarify points in our message.

A good presentation technique is to give the audience a couple of facts, which are then immediately followed up with a story. The story provides an example of the facts in the correct context, which has the effect of clarifying the point being made in the mind of the listener. We process stories in a different part of the brain from facts and so this helps us to absorb material more readily. We also tend to visualise stories in our 'mind's eye' and this too causes us to make more sense of the facts being presented.

This technique is increasingly being used in business as a strategic communication tool. One of the finest exponents of storytelling for use in business is Doug Stevenson. Doug has a background in both acting and business and has pulled his experience and strengths together to become an outstanding speaker and coach. He is based in Colorado Springs in the USA and is known for his Story Theatre presentation seminar. Not only is this workshop a fine example of Seminar Selling in itself, it is a fabulous opportunity to discover how to integrate story telling into your business communications. I would strongly recommend it to any small business looking for new and creative ways to increase sales.

Another presenter who is a brilliant storyteller is Tim Gard from the USA. Humour is at the heart of his presentations, but his humour is simply a series of observational stories. Check out Tim on YouTube to see what I mean.

The best type of stories are those which involve you and your personal backstory. Humans are hardwired to listen to stories – in particular those where people have overcome problems and adversity. They are often known as Epiphany Stories, and typically describe how you were going down a particular road in life but kept coming up against a brick wall.

Eventually through hard work, luck or whatever, you 'saw the light' and progressed quickly – and so became the person you are today.

That is a very short description of an Epiphany Story, but hopefully you can understand the structure.

What personal stories could you tell in your presentations that would help people to get to know you, empathise with you and which are an analogy for a point you are trying to get across?

I guarantee that when your presentations tell stories such as this, interest in you, your products, your expertise and your services will increase dramatically. What's more, you will open new doors to other speaking work because people will want to hire you to tell your story at their own event or organisation.

In summary, clarity is vital within your presentation. It is so easy to get completely wrapped up in the message you are trying to get across and completely forget about the audience. When planning your presentation material, take off your blinkers and get a very clear idea of what you want to say and then brainstorm different ways of saying it.

Don't just assume that you should automatically run a PowerPoint presentation. Are there other, more creative ways of getting your message across which will be more readily understood by the audience? And whatever you do, keep it simple, clear and efficient and think carefully about the image of your business that you want to convey. If the audience sees clutter and chaos, that is the image of your business that they will take away.

If they see clarity, efficiency and someone who cares about them, they will be far more disposed to doing business with you.

Conviction

"Presentation is everything. But substance and content is vital."

Rt Hon Margaret Beckett MP

As I write the updated version of this book, we are into the third year of discussion, debate, arguments and negotiations over Brexit, the scheduled withdrawal of the United Kingdom from the European Union.

Barely a day has gone by without there being extensive coverage on TV, radio and social media. It has sewn deep divisions amongst communities and families, and the public has lost a huge amount of faith in British politics.

Politicians have become far more aggressive in tone and the debate has done very little to enhance the perception of members of Parliament as being able to represent their constituents' interests.

Conviction has been replaced by bloody mindedness.

Conviction was once an essential characteristic of politicians and top presenters, and should convey the perception of enthusiasm, trust, belief, self-assurance and principal. Although we have mentioned passion on a number of occasions, it is worthless without conviction as this helps to reinforce the perception of your expertise.

Passion on its own can be infectious, but it does not work for everyone in an audience and each attendee at your seminar or workshop must believe that you are sincere as well. Conviction is something that either you have, or you haven't, and it could be argued that it is something you can't train into people. Nevertheless, presenters should be aware of its importance.

Characteristics of Presenters with Conviction

There are several characteristics of good presenters who display conviction.

- Presenters with conviction rarely appear to be 'selling' their product or service in their presentations. Their enthusiasm and expertise are apparent to all and this is usually sufficient to convince attendees of the quality of your main product.

- Presenters with conviction are skilful at pitching their level of expertise at just the right level with audiences. They appear to be able to read audiences well and neither patronise them nor go too far over their heads.

- Presenters with conviction will make minimal use of notes. Notes, while being useful, are really a crutch for the presenter and those who know their subject well (and who have bothered to thoroughly rehearse) will be less likely to use them to any great degree. Again, the amount you use notes or a script will help to determine the audience's perception of expertise.

- Those who do not use notes and scripts usually adopt a more conversational tone in the delivery of their presentation. This makes them look more 'human' and more authoritative – something to which audiences are inevitably attracted.

- Look people in the eye. There are various schools of thought on where you should look when addressing an audience. Some trainers say you should find a spot on the back of the hall or room and use that as a 'marker' so that your voice will be clear to everyone. I tend to take the view that if you care about each and every member of the audience, you will make every effort to address each one of them. There is no better way in my book than by looking people in the eye – and for that moment to speak directly to that person.

  None of us trust people who don't look us in the eye when they are talking to us, so why should it be any different in a presentation – particularly one where the presenter is trying to convince people of their expertise?

- When using stories as part of the presentation, try to use examples from your own personal experience and ideally stories of a personal adversity. Again, this creates an image of humility and gives extra credibility to your message.

We can all think of examples of television personalities who are really passionate about their subject and although they are people who are occasionally considered as perhaps less glamorous, cool or sexy than some other celebrities, they are often felt to be much more sincere.

Love or hate the never-ending conveyor belt of cookery programmes, you can't fail to be impressed by the celebrity chefs' technical expertise, dedication, confidence and heartfelt belief in what they do.

Perhaps Mrs Beckett's quotation should have been:

"Presentation is everything. But substance, content *and conviction* is vital."

Connection

"We can only connect through trust. People trust referrals from other people who've had a good experience with your organisation.

Following scandals such as Enron, Worldcom and Andersen, most organisations are rightly focusing on a psychological turnaround. They are spending time developing trust with their staff, customers and suppliers.

How are you building trust? What are people saying about you? Do you know? Is it contributing positively or negatively to your organisations success?"

Marie Mosley, Business psychologist, international speaker and broadcaster

Connecting with members of the audience or group is about chemistry and relationships. The two need to go hand in hand.

However, relationships need to be worked on and nurtured, but unfortunately for you, unless your seminar has an audience made up of close friends and family, you will have a lot of work to do to get the relationships up to speed quickly, so that people will be interested, excited and ready to hang on your every word. We mentioned earlier the importance of meeting and greeting every attendee, and this is the first step in this very important relationship building process.

As well as introducing yourself, try to introduce people to other people so that conversation builds. The sound of conversation in a room when people arrive helps them to feel more inclined to participate, as the last thing you want is silence. Background music on arrival also helps to relax people and make them feel welcome (remember – you need a license to do this or check to see if your venue has one that covers you).

Make sure that everyone has a badge with their name and if appropriate, the name of their business. You'll find this of as much benefit to you as them, particularly when making introductions. Ask one of your helpers to stand behind the registration table to welcome people and give them their badge.

Lay out the badges on the table with the names *facing the helper*. You want the badge to be found as quickly as possible as this helps people to feel that they are expected. The delegate will still spot their name even if it is upside down, so together with the helper viewing them the right way up the badge will quickly be found.

Treat the period when people are arriving a bit like a cocktail party – get them talking and interacting. All your focus should now be on them and under no circumstances should you concern yourself with projectors, flipcharts, notes or any other mechanics of your presentation.

We discovered that a little light humour directed at yourself will also help to oil the wheels. The warmth you create during this opening twenty minutes before your presentation is crucial to the degree to which you connect with people when you start talking, so make sure you put in the effort so that they are as receptive as possible to you.

Getting Started

When your seminar starts, try to have someone else introduce you. This is not vital, but it does help to build your credibility right from the start and set the right atmosphere.

It doesn't matter who does the introduction for you, just as long as you give them a script, and they practice reading it for several days beforehand. It also doesn't matter if they read it when introducing you, and because they probably will read it rather than learn it, print the introduction in large, clear type. The script shouldn't be too long, flamboyant or include too many of your achievements – just a few well-chosen words to start things up.

Whilst we agree that impact is vital at the start, concentrate on making a *friendly* impact. Feel free to burst onto the stage like the Rolling Stones but ensure you make an impact for the right reasons. You must be seen at this early stage as friendly, personable and approachable, so that people subconsciously think 'I like this person'.

Here are a few more ideas to help you connect with the audience:

- Walk with purpose and look positive and optimistic.

- Actively listen to people when they speak to you on arrival. Look them in the eye and *really listen hard*.

- Don't stand behind a lectern at the early stages (ideally, don't stand behind a lectern at all).

- Ask people at the back if they can see and hear you.

- Ask people if they are too hot or too cold.

- Reassure people that they can get up and move about if they are uncomfortable.

- Make an observation about something local that they would have heard about – like the new traffic lights down the road, or the weather.

- Tell the audience that you have been looking forward to the event.

- When someone asks a question, repeat it for the benefit of the room because not everyone might have heard it clearly, and then answer it to the whole room. When you have finished answering the question, ask the questioner if that helped them.

- Above all, smile.

Trial Closes

A really important tip to improve connection and dramatically increase the likelihood of people wanting to talk to you afterwards – or indeed purchase your back of room products is to use Trial Closes.

Throughout your presentation you want to get the audience nodding their heads as if agreeing with you or saying Yes to questions that you ask.

You should start doing this right from the very beginning of the presentation – even during your opening remarks. For example, if it's a really cold day outside and there is snow in the air, start by saying something that you know everyone will agree with. You could say something like,

"Wow, it's cold today isn't it?!".

You could emphasis the point by wrapping your arms around yourself as if trying to keep warm.

The chances are that everyone in the room will nod and agree with you.

Or you could say something like,

"Isn't this an amazing venue?!"

What we're trying to do is to get everyone nodding and agreeing with you right from the start.

Then as your presentation progresses, occasionally ask questions such as,

"Does what I just said make sense?"
"Does that sound good?"
"Is that OK?"
"Isn't that amazing?!"
"Do you understand what I'm trying to say?"
"Does that sound fair?"
"Do you follow me so far?"
"Can you see how much time that would save?"
"Can you see how this would make your life easier?"
"Can you see how that would work?"
"Can you start to visualise yourself doing that?"
"It's an interesting angle on this, don't you agree?"
"You've probably heard about this approach, right?"
"Would you like to learn the loophole?"

"We're really excited about this new development and I imagine many of you are too?"
"That sounds like a valid approach to this, yes?"

And so on. Modify these to suit your personal presentation style and the content of your presentation.

This is a little-known technique used by people who sell from the stage, and it works. It's been proven to dramatically increase your chances of people wanting to talk to you afterwards and buy your products – particularly if you make a point of inviting people to talk to you.

"Would anyone like to ask me a question in private?"
"Would anyone be interested in taking a closer look at my book?"
"Would anyone like to make an appointment with me today?"
"Would anyone like to buy a bottle right now?"

And as you ask the question, gently nod your head as if saying Yes.

Whilst this approach is very effective, I would definitely not always advocate going for a sale at every presentation that you give. If your presentation has focused on your value, credibility and expertise, you will find that people will want to talk to you anyway, if not buy something there and then. What's more, simply asking people if they want an appointment or to purchase something has to be done in a very professional way which we'll come on to. There is a technique to it.

Use the Trial Closes throughout your presentation primarily to keep people on side with you. If nothing else, the audience's answers to your questions will confirm whether or not they really are agreeing with you.

There are also specific points in your presentation when you might want to use a Trial Close. For example, when transitioning from one topic or theme to another. At the end of a section ask the audience something like *"Did that make sense to everyone?"* before moving on.

Secondly, include a Trial Close after explaining a specific feature or benefit – *"Do you agree that sounds valuable?"*

Finally, if you are highlighting a testimonial from a happy client/customer during your presentation, you could say something like *"Wow, isn't that exciting?!"*

You can also use Trial Closes after testimonials or features and benefits in the promotional materials for your event.

Two words of caution when using Trial Closes during your presentations:

- Don't overdo it, or it could come over as 'forced' and some people will feel that you are being too salesy. What we're trying to do is get to a point where people feel that it is the most natural thing in the world to want to talk to you afterwards, without feeling that they have been sold to.

- If you are speaking overseas, check that nodding means that someone is in agreement with you.

    I discovered this when speaking in Bulgaria, when a nodding audience means the exact opposite. Audiences in India also do not necessarily nod when agreeing with something you say, so do your research first.

Should I include external expert speakers?

At some seminars, particularly events that last several hours, the host will (not surprisingly) arrange for an additional speaker to make a contribution. In Financial Services, a regular speaker who fills this slot is Justin Urquhart Stewart of Seven Investment Management.

In many ways this is good as it provides added value for the audience; on the other hand, you run the risk of them being a better speaker or more charismatic than yourself. Even worse is if the audience warms more to them than you – which often happens when financial advisers invite Justin to come and speak!

The worst-case scenario is that the audience perceive the other speaker to be more of an expert than you. This could result in people gravitating to the other speaker at the end of the event and worse still, buying that person's back of the room product instead of your own!

As we have said before, the whole point of seminars and workshops is to provide a forum or platform for you to demonstrate your expertise. You don't want your seminar becoming a platform for someone else.

The right way to deal with this, is to put your guest speaker on early (perhaps before a coffee break) so they can do their thing and then leave. You, the host, should always be the final speaker.

Staying Connected

Staying connected with people throughout your event is just as important. Make sure you have regular breaks, whether it is for tea, coffee and comfort breaks or even for people to get some fresh air. Some people will want anything but fresh air, but whatever the reason, stop and let people out regularly.

When you are dealing with a complex part of the presentation, perhaps involving numbers or statistics, try to keep these passages short.

After any period which has needed intense concentration, immediately follow it with either a formal break or lighten things up considerably with your tone, pace, moving about, saying something amusing (about yourself) or completely changing the subject. In fact, regularly changing the pace and tone of your talk is to be recommended anyway as it helps to keep people awake and alert.

However passionate you are about your subject, don't ever get to the point where you run the risk of irritating people. Most will be impressed with your knowledge and expertise but do allow room for other people's views. After all, they have decided to attend your seminar because they have interest in your subject, so it is very likely that they will have their own thoughts and ideas.

Even if you are the world's leading authority on a subject, always listen with interest and respect to what people in your audience have to say, and never argue – even if they are irritating you!

Equally, do not ever underestimate your audience. There are always people present who know more about the subject than you think. If you ever talk down to them you're in for trouble.

After the Event

It is just as important to keep the connection going immediately *after* your talk as before and during it. If you have back of room products, this is the point when you need to be at your most charming.

Even if people have already decided that they will purchase your book or course or whatever, it helps to reassure them of the wisdom of making the purchase if they can briefly talk to you in person. You may even find that they would like it signed. Write their name in the book as well but check the spelling first.

Sometimes you will find a queue of people waiting to talk to you. For this reason it is useful to have helpers who can sell your products for you. Although you want to sell products, it's important that you spend time talking to people – some will want to talk to you for 20 minutes or more! I'm not exaggerating when I say that I have spent over two hours talking to people after an event or presentation and it never ceases to amaze me how long people will wait to talk to you.

You must still be seen as friendly and approachable as this is something that people will tell all their friends and business associates about.

Part 3

What Happens Next?

Getting Feedback

"My entire perspective on the business of sales and marketing is coloured by my being transgender.

It amazes me how as a man I failed to see just how little attention businesses pay to the fact that a significant growing number of their buyers are women. 85% of consumer payments are made by women, 45% of the workforce are women, marketing and buying departments are predominantly staffed by women, 40% of new businesses are owned by women.

Yet most advertising and marketing is based on male communication strategies. To succeed in sales and marketing in the next decade small business owners will need to look hard at how to reach their female buyers."

Rikki Arundel,
Professional Speaker, GenderShift.com

So you have reached the point where the big day has come and gone. And hopefully you will already have won new clients. They may be customers for your new back of room products, or your main product or service. You may even have had people ask you to provide high value coaching or consultancy services.

You should also have found new friends who will be great advocates for your business and who will be busy spreading the word about your seminar or your expertise.

You will also find that more people will be visiting your website where they can find out more information about your main products and services.

This is all fantastic news, but it's important now to be thinking of the next step and looking for ways to improve both your content and delivery for future events. The best way to do this is to ask the attendees, from whom you will obtain both formal and informal feedback.

Formal Feedback

Although I am not a fan of 'Happy Sheets', the best way to obtain feedback from delegates is to ask them to complete a post-event questionnaire. This should be given to them on the day as part of your closing comments.

Keep it to just one side of a sheet of paper and ask questions which provide you with practical advice with which to improve your event. It is always nice to have comments which say how good the event was, but you should be thinking of the future. Include by all means questions which will produce responses which could be used in future marketing materials but focus on improvement.

You also want these attendees to help you with the marketing for your next event, so ask them to include the names of other people they know who might benefit from the seminar or workshop. Wherever possible, try to get contact details.

As well as giving you referrals for future events, you can also ask if people would be interested in helping you to promote future events as an agent or affiliate of yours. Make it clear that you will reward them for their efforts.

Your questions could include some of the following:

- How, specifically, have you benefited from today's seminar?
- How will you use the information you have been given?
- How will the event affect your productivity?
- How could the event be improved for the benefit of future attendees?
- What would you include that was not covered today?
- Was there anything that should have been left out?
- Which was the most enjoyable or useful part of the presentation?
- Was there anything that was unclear?
- Was there anything of particular interest on which you would like further information?
- What comments do you have on the venue?
- Was it convenient for you to get to?

- Is there a different venue that would be preferable to you?

- Were there any problems that we should be aware of in future?

- Was the time of the event convenient for you? Do you have any suggestions in this regard?

- To what extent would you recommend this seminar to friends and colleagues?

- Are there any products or services which we currently do not offer, which could be of use to you in future?

- Please would you consider providing the names of three people who you think we should approach?

- What is the best way to contact you so that we can send any updates or supplementary information?

As you can see, all these questions are designed to illicit information which can be used to your benefit. You may also want to include a final question which asks attendees to write a general comment on the day.

A catch-all question that I use is:

"What would you say to someone who is thinking about attending this event?"

The answers to this often give you a lot of valuable information. Quite often the answers are written in a way which make an ideal testimonial. Ask the person's permission to use their comment in future marketing materials.

And on the subject of testimonials, as mentioned earlier, immediately after your event – while you are still in the room is the perfect time to get a video testimonial. If you are standing talking to someone who has clearly enjoyed your event, make a point of politely asking them if they could say just a few words on camera.

As was the case on all your promotional material, remember to include your email and website address on your feedback form. Although most people hand it in there and then, some do not so you need to give them another chance to send it back separately.

If anyone asks a question on the post event form, make absolutely sure that you reply immediately. A week afterwards is too late – try to make it the day after your talk. And a great way to respond is by using video email.

Your formal feedback is vital – just make sure that you use it.

Informal Feedback

Informal feedback is made up of snippets of information you pick up on the day of the event both before, during and immediately afterwards.

Keep a notebook with you on the day to write down anything that is said to you or that you overhear. Make a note too of the questions that people ask so that you can be better prepared in future. If you have helpers with you ask them to also keep notes of anything which came to mind.

Put a shortened version of the feedback form on your website to enable people to make any comments or additional points. This should be included on a special page which only attendees can visit. On the day of your event, give people a note of the address of the special web page and explain that only seminar attendees have access to it. Set up the page so that it requires a password to access and make a point of giving out the password to people in a sealed envelope at the end of the event. By offering a special web page you you're your attendees feel special and the sealed envelope adds an extra air of mystery.

Also on this page there will be a summary of the topics covered in the seminar (even though they may have been given a workbook or taken notes), together with supplementary information. Provide choice in the way people can feed back information through your website by giving both an email address they could use and a form with boxes they can fill in. Another option is to give people a link to a survey that they can complete, using a tool such as SurveyMonkey. A nice touch is to give people an Amazon voucher or similar as an incentive.

The special webpage needs to be live on the day of the event itself as some people will go straight back home and immediately log onto your site.

Summary

If you have had a number of helpers or colleagues involved in your event and they are all present on the day, arrange a debrief meeting within half an hour of the last delegate leaving.

You will all, I assure you, be extremely elated and tired. Very tired! But it is your first impressions that really count. Your tiredness will help you to remember the things that did not go well or needed improvement and your elation will help you to recall what went well. Write down your thoughts and add them to the information gained through the feedback forms, your notes and any comments which come in via your website.

As a final point, consider asking five delegates if they would be interested in providing more detailed feedback. Choose a cross section of attendees and ask if they would be willing to either complete a more detailed feedback form or take part in a one-to-one interview with you where you go through each section of the event.

In some cases you might wish to consider filming or recording these interviews as they will help you to remember the detail later. With permission, you may even be able to use snippets of the interviews in future marketing materials or include them on a recording of the event itself for later sale.

Yes – even your feedback can be turned into profits!

Following Up to Maximise Sales and Profits

"Word-of-mouth marketing is the easiest and most cost-effective way to increase sales. We are a gossip species. Human beings talk about each other.

When we encourage those we know to do it proactively, we dramatically increase the effectiveness of word-of-mouth marketing."

Roy Sheppard, International Speaker & Moderator
Rapid Results Referrals

There really is no point running seminars and workshops unless you follow up afterwards. However, whenever I attend a seminar, there is often no follow up at all, and when there is, it is too late.

You have gone to great lengths to put on a high quality, high value event which will hopefully have impressed your delegates or attendees.

You will have gathered some useful feedback and will already be working on your next event. But now is the time to pull it all together.

Following your debrief meeting you can go to the bar to relax. You deserve it. But the next day you have work to do.

The Next Day

Just as you have planned the content and promotion of your event, you should also plan your follow up. Remember to refer to your overall objectives for the events and plan the follow up accordingly. Decide exactly what you are going to do to follow up and when.

One thing you must do is send out pre-prepared follow-up letters (not emails) to each attendee.

Allow room to add in any special remarks which reflect anything particularly interesting or amusing that happened or was said during the day. Also, find the answers to any questions which you were not able to answer. It is very important to answer questions immediately as this adds to your credibility.

It would be even more impressive if you were able to send out these letters on the day of the event itself so that they arrive the following morning. This is normally quite difficult to achieve, but well worth it if you can manage it. Hand write the salutation, and also include a handwritten 'PS' – something simple like *"Great to see you and looking forward to catching up again very soon"*

A novel and distinctive approach is to send a follow up text message on the day of the event. Naturally, keep it short! You'll be surprised just how many will respond.

Contact anyone who was not able to attend and send an appropriate letter. Offer them a further incentive to either attend a future event or a discount on your products (either back of room or your main product/service). You may even wish to give them access to the special website complete with the relevant password.

On the day of your seminar you may have also told all your attendees that you are holding a draw for everyone who attended. Pick the winner the next day and personally deliver the prize.

As we saw earlier from Clive Thompson at Serenity Financial Planning, send a press release to the local papers summarising the event but write it in a way which explains how attendees benefited and include information about future events which you may be holding. Ask one of your helpers to take a photograph of you at the seminar and include it with your release.

If you filmed or recorded your seminar, now is the time to be editing and packaging your video. Ask your web designer to use clips on your website which visitors can watch or listen to.

Closer Analysis

As part of your follow-up process you will be analysing all the feedback from the event and starting to take the necessary steps to make improvements for next time. The feedback is important as it could directly impact the profitability of future events.

Typically, closer analysis will reveal problems as follows:

- Not enough time given to the planning of the event. Yes, you may have allocated five months as described earlier, but distractions inevitably slow things down.

- Not having clear enough objectives that are written down.

- Not targeting the content of the event closely enough at the needs or problems of attendees.

- Not promoting the event in a broad enough range of media.

- Not providing sufficient options for people to make further enquiries or to respond.

- Not providing sufficient incentive to attend.

- Not highlighting sufficient benefits of attending.

- Not making the event irresistible to people in your target market.

During the event, analysis of feedback will reveal some of the following:

- Possible equipment failure or tech issues.

- Overuse and poor use of PowerPoint.

- Not being sufficiently friendly, relaxed, enthusiastic, cheerful or inspirational.

- Lack of rehearsal.

- Not providing what was advertised.

- Holding back the 'meat' of your knowledge and expertise.

- Not sharing some of your content and images of the day on Social Media.

- Lack of attention to maintaining a strong connection with the audience (i.e. building relationships and keeping them alert at all times).

After the event a common problem is not following up on promises made during the presentation. If you tell someone that you will get back to them with an answer to their query, make sure that you do. Nothing is worse for denting your credibility.

Maximising Sales and Profits

As time passes and you have held several events you will develop your own ways to plan and prepare your events.

You will discover your own ways of promoting the events and the best ways of doing so within your target market. You will also be building an impressive list of contacts who have opted-in to receive details of additional products and services.

Just as your seminars do not seek to overtly promote your products or service, neither should your follow-up activities. Your promotional activities should always aim to highlight your expertise, from which prospects can draw their own conclusions.

Your email newsletter should be at the heart of your follow-up activities, by providing regular, valuable hints, tips and advice for people interested in your business, products and services. The newsletter must provide real value, or it will soon be consigned to the recycle bin.

It has four main objectives:

1. To keep in touch with your clients and prospects.

2. To regularly send people to your website.

3. To remind people of your expertise and the quality of your service.

4. To advise people of future events.

Driving People to your Website

For people who attend your seminars, you want your website to act as an alternative place to experience your business.

You can use this piece of cyberspace to build on ideas in your newsletter and to provide additional information not covered at your seminar.

For those who attended your seminar, your website gives another opportunity to promote your back of room products, in particular your information-based products which can be sold in electronic format.

As we said earlier, eBooks can be extremely profitable as they only need to be produced once. A number of professional speakers sell multiple eBooks via their websites after their seminars or conference presentations and use their email newsletter as their main method to remind conference attendees of their content and expertise.

Many will tell you that someone needs to visit your website four to six times at which point they will purchase a product online. And there is evidence to show that the same person will visit your website again in the month following and will make another purchase.

So you can see that if you have a tool that is encouraging people to visit your website on a regular basis, there is a strong likelihood that this will pay dividends, particularly in the days and weeks immediately after your seminars and events. Don't forget, each eBook you sell is pure profit.

Make eBooks tangible

It's quite one thing for someone to visit your website and to see details about an information product that you have written. But unlike books in a bookshop you can't pick them up, touch them, smell them and read a few paragraphs, so how do you expect people to be attracted to them?

Again, this is where your seminar comes in. People who have seen you 'live' and witnessed your expertise at first hand will have been given all the information they would ever need to decide whether they want to buy your eBook. Similarly, this is another reason why your email newsletter has to be of high value. People will have already read a great deal of your work and will have come to their own conclusions about the likely value of your product.

But a great way to reinforce the message is to give your eBook a 'real' cover. Software is available for you to design a sleeve which can then be put on your website. It actually looks like the cover of a real book, complete with your name and title and so enhances the perceived value of the product. To make your eBook look even more 'real', the software creates the cover in 3D to make it look as though it is standing on a shelf.

Reminder of your Expertise

Assuming you delivered high value and high content at your seminars, your email newsletter will help you to reinforce your expertise. But it must at all costs be worth the virtual paper it is printed on. If your recipients are satisfied that it is of value to them, you will have a friend and very often, a customer for life.

These recipients will buy your products, participate in surveys and competitions and will even travel long distances to attend your talks.

It is also the case that not everyone who attends your seminars or workshops wants to buy anything at all from you! But they just might in future, so you want to make sure that when they are ready to buy something, they come to you first. It is possible for many recipients of your email newsletter to stay quiet for months or years without ever communicating with you. It doesn't mean they don't read or enjoy your communications – just keep in touch and one day they will come.

You also recall from earlier in this book that you can make money from the email newsletter itself by offering a 'premium' version which people have to pay for.

Naturally the content will need to be of higher value, and you will find that a great many of your 'fans' will be more than happy to upgrade. Apart from anything else, the curiosity alone will have its appeal.

Information on Future Events

As well as profits from your seminars themselves, consultancy activities, back of room products, website/eBook sales and email newsletter upgrades, you also have the option of advertising future events and offering Premium Seminars.

Sometimes known as Bootcamps or Retreats, Premium Seminars take your events to the next level, and I believe they are a golden opportunity for financial advisers. They provide you with a platform to offer a workshop for those clients or prospects who are looking for more exclusive, higher value material which is perhaps more appropriate to their needs.

Such events are often held over a weekend at a prestigious and comfortable venue and invariably will be at a price which reflects the quality of the event. Given the location you may also want to include a more social aspect in the agenda and schedule in time for delegates to make use of a variety of leisure facilities.

Not surprisingly, if you charge anything from seven hundred to several thousand pounds, the profits from these events can be substantial, particularly if you have a wide range of back of room products available for purchase.

Finally, don't be scared to send out email. I've talked about this a lot in this book and I know that some readers will be nervous about 'annoying' their list by seemingly sending out too much.

In fact, many top internet marketers will confirm that the number of products you sell through your email promotions, is in direct proportion to the amount of email you send out.

I discovered this myself when I first started emailing my financial adviser contacts who had joined my online group.

I started out sending an email newsletter once every two weeks, and sure enough I always got people responding positively in some way, shape or form.

A friend in the tech space asked me why I didn't send out an email to my list more often, to which I told him that I was worried that I would simply be seen as annoying.

He told me that was nonsense and suggested that I go from sending out an email newsletter once every two weeks to *every day*.

I had genuine doubts about doing this but decided to trial it for a month – and so went from sending out my newsletter twice a month to thirty-one times a month!

The impact was startling. Yes, I got a handful of unsubscribers, but the number of daily visits to my online group went off the charts, as did enquiries for my eBooks and workshops.

All serious internet marketers say the same thing – send more email!

Clearly you have to be mindful of GDPR rules and what you send people, but work within what is allowed and you should see extremely positive returns.

Of course, you will get some unsubscribers, but arguably they may not be the clients you ultimately want. But keep your email newsletter full of value, a little humour and stories and anecdotes that are relevant to their needs, and your efforts will be well rewarded.

On several occasions throughout this book we have talked about the benefits of email newsletters. Fundamentally their main value is providing the small business owner with an inexpensive, quick, interactive, easy and efficient communication tool which can be used to not only provide information to clients and prospects, but to rapidly direct people to additional information.

Email is unrivalled in its ability to perform a variety of communication functions and whilst unwanted email can be a big problem, when used carefully, correctly and creatively it can be an extraordinarily powerful business tool. I urge you to explore its possibilities.

Some Final Thoughts

So there it is – Seminar Selling and Live Marketing is a powerful and proven promotional strategy for your financial advice business. For some readers it will be new, and for others I hope that I've given you some valuable insights into how you can take your events up a few gears.

Live Marketing and demonstration-based selling has always been extremely effective because it allows the prospect to see your product or service in action before they get out their wallet. But it's not just the demonstration that makes the difference. It's the ability of the prospect to go to a deeper level and gain a more detailed impression of the people behind the business. And in my view, this is critical for the financial advice profession.

Today's consumers are much more sophisticated than they were even a few years ago and with the help of the internet they are now able to compare hundreds of different products and services from the comfort of their own home. Indeed, the detail in which they can compare products is staggering. Every tiny piece of information that you might want is available immediately, and even if it isn't, it doesn't take long to find it.

Not surprisingly, many products are increasingly being commoditised as customers can not only compare product features but can quickly locate stores offering the lowest price.

So how do small businesses fight back?

Service is an obvious differentiator, but many businesses struggle to find ways of making their service both creative and innovative. Even more difficult is to convince customers in a leaflet or on a website that their service really does offer something special. After all, every brochure from every business in every part of the UK claims to offer service which is 'Second to none'.

How then can we *prove* to people that we really do have the edge and that we truly surprise and delight our clients?

By showing them.

By giving them a live demonstration of our expertise. By enabling clients and prospects to see, touch and experience what we do at a seminar, workshop, demonstration or social event.

What better way could there be to promote our product or service?

Businesses have always hosted these events and those that do know all too well how effective they can be. But far too many do not, and they are missing out. It's easily understandable why they do not, but I hope that this book will give them a few ideas.

The good news for them is that effective Seminar Selling is not just about putting on a nice talk and then waiting for the orders to roll in. When combined with today's incredible communication technology the possibilities are endless.

But it is the way that technology can be employed to market, support and follow up your events which is most exciting. Not only that, the very same technology that you use to promote your events can be used to create information products and produce incredible profits in their own right.

Successful Seminar Selling is a magical combination of substance, style and good old-fashioned face-to-face communication, skilfully blended with modern communication technology. It gives you a golden opportunity to stand out from the crowd and show clients what your business is really all about.

Grasp that opportunity with both hands today.

Good luck with your seminars, workshops and demonstrations – in fact *all* your promotional activities. Let me know how you get on!

Confessions of a Mystery Seminar Shopper

From time to time I'm asked to be a mystery shopper at clients' seminars, and I wanted to include in this book an example of how an event comes over to me as an attendee. What follows, nicely sums up many of the points made so far.

In this particular example, I was asked by the head office of a national firm of financial advisers to attend a seminar being hosted by advisers in one of their offices in Hampshire, UK.

I was to pretend to be a member of the public who was potentially interested in appointing the firm as my financial advisers, and was asked to report back to the head office marketing team with my feedback on everything that happened from receipt of the invitation through to the follow up I received. The local office did not know that I had been hired by their head office, so as far as they were concerned, I was a prospect just like anyone else in attendance.

The company was rolling out a series of nationwide events, and whilst the theme/topic of the seminars was the same around the UK, local offices could choose their own venue, personalise the invitations and decide on the format of the presentation itself. There were pre-prepared handouts and leaflets which local offices could give to attendees.

The Seminar Invitation

My invitation arrived on June 2nd. The envelope was high quality and my name and address were spelt correctly. The envelope was DL size (110mm x 220mm) and looked 'official' but not too official so I opened it with interest.

The letter had been sent second class and it included a nondescript postmark. Better would have been to send it first class and with a stamp – the inclusion of which adds to the impression that a human had been involved in its sending. Second class suggests that it might be a mailing letter, whereas first class hints at importance.

I opened the letter and pulled out four sheets of A4 which had been folded twice so that they fitted in the DL envelope. I was pleased to note that the first thing I saw was my name handwritten *Dear Mr Calvert*.

So far so good. Hand writing the salutation is very important if we are going to get people's attention, because it looks like we have put in some effort to make it personal.

The mailing letter was well written, though the overall message wasn't particularly trained on my specific needs – though they weren't to know what they were because I had been sneaked onto their invitation list. That said, I got the impression that the same letter had been sent to everyone on their list.

So the letter appeared to be more of an invitation to a talk/seminar which was more generic in nature than I and perhaps other recipients would have liked.

"You are invited to meet Jones & Co and to discover the latest developments in retirement income planning."

I then noticed the date of the event which was to be the 16th June – just fourteen days away.

By any standards that is short notice, and one of the main reasons why seminar hosts don't get a full house at their events. Couple that with the generic nature of the presentation, and those two points alone could put their event in jeopardy.

On the plus side, the letter included multiple reasons why I would benefit by attending – not least of which was the country house hotel venue and high-quality buffet lunch. I had not been to that particular hotel, so maybe that would pique my interest…

The letter went on to explain that the local regional manager would be speaking, along with two of his colleagues who were experts on the topic of retirement planning. The letter included the name of the regional manager, but not his colleagues - so I couldn't look them up on LinkedIn or elsewhere if I had wanted to.

It did say that the regional manager's name was Jim Williamson (not his real name) and there was a friendly photo of him. He looked a nice enough guy. It said that Jim has worked with Jones and Co for ten years, lived locally and was a regular at the tennis club.

All good stuff. Had I been a tennis player myself, I would certainly have edged a notch closer to my tipping point, but all the same this added a human touch to the doubtless technical world of retirement planning.

The remainder of the letter explained that in addition to the meat of the seminar (to be held between 11am and 2.30pm to include lunch) we would be introduced to Jones and Co's services. That's not the biggest draw of the event, but at least we would get to see and meet the people behind the expertise.

In addition, we got a photo of the venue, and a short list of the awards that it had won over the last few years – including a brief mention of the chef who had worked in a restaurant in London which had two Michelin stars. Now that got my attention.

I also noticed that on the reply-paid card I could opt to book a 'Hot Seat'.

This is something that you quite often see at seminars in the USA but not often in the UK. Although the Jones and Co event was free to attend, I could 'upgrade' and purchase a Hot Seat which meant that I would have a guaranteed space at the front and would be sat with our hosts over lunch. I figured that some people would definitely take up that option.

I mentally gave them a Bonus Point for this because they were clearly thinking with a commercial mind and adding in higher perceived value.

Already we can see how important the mailer can be. Whilst essentially it is there to promote the event, different aspects of its contents will appeal to different people – so it's important to think very carefully about what to include.

Many people will tell you that the mailing letter should stick to just one side of A4 in order to keep it brief. I understand that brevity is important, but more so is including everything that could possibly influence people to attend. In the glory days of direct response marketing before the internet came along, it was not unknown for sales letters to have twenty or more pages! Even today, many top internet marketers will include sales pages for products on their websites which seemingly go on forever.

Why do they do it like that? Because it works!

Included in the seminar invitation letter was a reply-paid postcard, already completed with my name – all I needed to do was to tick that I was going to attend and pop it in the post. I noticed that there was a named individual in Jones and Co's address which I took note of just in case I had any questions before the event.

A reply-paid postcard is OK, but they could have given me at least three more ways to respond – usually any of these:

- Email
- Phone
- On a special page on their website
- Text
- Facebook Messenger
- WhatsApp
- Twitter
- Etc.

In the old days we would have also included Fax.

Finally, the letter was hand-signed, but there was no PS. I've seen some research that suggests people always read the PS even if they miss out parts of the main body of the letter. That may or may not be true, but the PS gives you a last chance to get your main benefit across in a short and punchy sentence, and most internet marketers I know get quite creative with their PS – so use it.

For me, the mailing letter had some good elements, but missed several opportunities to make it even better. Again, these missed opportunities could mean fewer people attending than you had hoped.

I sent back my reply-paid card and waited for the event. In the meantime, I went online to check out Jones and Co and also the venue. Don't forget this point, because after reading your promotional piece – whether sent as a letter or email, people will inevitably want to check you out further if they are interested.

Between sending my card back and the date of the event itself, I didn't hear back from Jones and Co. That was a shame because a) I would have liked reassurance of my place and b) they missed an opportunity to engage with me.

As mentioned earlier in this book, this would have been a good opportunity for the event host to call me up, thank me for confirming my attendance and to ask me if I had any questions. The event host could also have asked if I would be happy to be included in a case study, if that was being included.

Calling me up would also have broken the ice before the event. Assuming we had a pleasant chat on the phone, the human connection would have been made and when I arrived at the venue we would already feel that we knew each other.

The Day of the Seminar

The directions to the venue were well written and accurate, even though I did use Sat Nav. The roads were clear though I didn't feel that it was particularly quiet that day, so this was a good choice of venue for access.

The country house hotel had an impressive driveway and the sun was out. There was a large parking area out front and I noticed a couple of Peacocks strutting about on the lawn.

Clearly some thought had been given to the venue. As I got out of my car, I stepped onto pea shingle which added a quality crunch underfoot. I don't know what it is about pea shingle drives, but they certainly add something to the ambience of the place.

I entered through the front door and found myself in a long corridor with reception to my left. Although I could have gone to reception, I would have liked to have immediately seen some sort of notice that pointed to the room where the seminar was being held. Although I knew I was in the right place, it is still a good touch to have an official notice. A pull-up banner would also be a good touch.

I went to the desk and asked for directions to the Jones and Co seminar, and a perfectly pleasant and cheerful young man leant over and pointed me further down the corridor.

Having been to multiple workshops, conferences and events over the years, my memory banks immediately recalled a seminar I attended once by American Management guru and author of *In Search of Excellence* Tom Peters. Tom spent a good hour at his seminar telling the audience about how he has trained countless hotel staff to "never point, always show", and that such a little thing can make a huge difference to a hotel guest's experience.

Clearly the member of staff at this hotel had missed this critical element of customer service.

Nevertheless, I wandered down the corridor and could shortly hear jazz music coming from the room I had been directed to.

I went into the room, which was bright and airy and which had large glass doors open to the lawn. A few other guests were mingling. The room felt welcoming.

Which was more than could be said for the member of staff from Jones and Co who, whilst standing right next to the door seemed very preoccupied with a clipboard and a list of names.

I waited a good fifteen seconds before he looked up, even though it was as clear as day that I had just walked into the room.

If I was giving out points for the day's experience so far, they would have got full marks up to the point of walking into the hotel, but then lost a few because of the lack of notice or sign, the poor engagement from the person on the desk and then the lack of welcome and attention in the seminar room.

"What is your name please?" came the question as the man on the door finally looked up. More points lost.

There was no *"Hi!"* or *"Good morning"* – just straight into the details he wanted so that he could put a tick by my name.

We did exchange a handshake and couple of pleasantries, and after giving me a sticky paper badge with my name on (not good), he got a couple of points back by offering to pour me a coffee.

He then surprised me and got even more points back by appearing to have a reserved seat for me.

"Ah yes, Mr Calvert – we have a place reserved for you over here..."

I wondered if he had been tipped off by his head office that I was attending as a mystery shopper, but quickly realised that he hadn't. I noticed that about fifteen percent of the seats in the room had Reserved signs on them – but none with actual names.

So what it appeared they were doing, was occasionally selecting guests at random who looked as though they would appreciate being treated with a bit more priority. How they chose which guests to select was unclear, but I thought it was a great tactic – and one that I suggest to clients. Bonus points given out for that one.

The Presentation

The room started to fill up, and the jazz background music created a great atmosphere. It was the first time I had heard jazz being used at any event and it worked well – and it had clearly been chosen specially by the organisers.

All too often, background music on arrival is forgotten altogether, which can make for an awkward silence if people don't talk. Otherwise hotel venues tend to have bland pop music which only serves to make the experience for guests a bit samey.

I once attended a seminar where they had a professional harpist, which was great – if ever so slightly over the top. But the jazz worked well.

As I browsed the agenda for the presentation I was tapped on the shoulder, to come face to face with our host Jim Williamson.

He glanced down at my badge and said,

"Mr Calvert, thank you so much for coming along today – I hope that you'll find it interesting."

Jim left it at that, which meant that it was my turn to say something. Given that I didn't know anything about Jim, the best I could come up with was to ask how his tennis was…

The ice broke and it felt as though I had been appointed as Jim's best friend.

If you are the host of an event, it's you that has to put in the effort to create social chit chat. All you need to do is to ask a question like *"Where have you come from today?"* and that will get your guests talking. Nevertheless, Jim got a bonus point for taking the trouble to say hello.

Jim then went to the front of the room, smiled broadly and welcomed us all.

After thanking everyone for giving up their time, he put up a slide with the order of play. Not strictly necessary because there was a printed agenda on our chairs, but the design of the first slide is usually a clue as to the quality of the presentation that is to come, and whether or not you're going to need binoculars.

This slide had large, clear text and was easy to read, even from the back of the room. So far, so good – hopefully we weren't going to get 'death by PowerPoint'.

We talked earlier in this book about Trial Closing, and whilst Jim's introduction was friendly and upbeat (he was clearly a confident and experienced presenter), he missed the opportunity to get us all nodding our heads in agreement. The opportunity he missed was to say something like,

"Wow, isn't this a fantastic venue – do you like it?!"

Without doubt, every person in the room would have said and nodded *"Yes!"*

I won't bore you with details of our presentation on 'the latest developments in retirement income planning', suffice to say that it was clear, delivered on its promise and left me knowing more than I knew when I arrived. I also felt that whilst I could probably have found the same information online, the fact that Jim and his team were presenting it live, enhanced the sense of trust and credibility that would be needed if I was to engage Jones and Co's services.

All that was missing for me were a couple of case studies – ideally involving people in the audience.

The Close

Jones and Co's seminar went off without a hitch; it was well presented and above all, there was a great atmosphere in the room. Jim and his colleagues had rehearsed and there were no technical issues.

As he wound up proceedings before lunch, there was very little by way of a sales pitch. In some ways that was a good thing, because they did a good enough job that attendees would naturally want to talk with Jim and his team afterwards – indeed, my estimate was a conversion rate on the day of approximately fifty percent which is quite respectable.

I felt though that this could have been higher if Jim had included more of a call to action. This doesn't have to be a salesy call to action, but he could have created more of a sense of urgency by highlighting that if people did want to work with them, they only had capacity to take on a limited number of new clients.

He could also have used an element of social proof by explaining how attendees at previous events had gone on to become clients. Sometimes it's a good idea to invite some existing clients to the event, who, with their prior permission could be pointed out if people wanted to talk to them.

Finally, at the back of the room there were copies of Jones and Co's *Guide to Increasing Income in retirement – A Special Report*.

This was a high quality, professionally produced document of about thirty pages. I glanced through it and it was definitely the sort of thing that made an excellent giveaway for attendees. Interestingly, the Special Report wasn't mentioned in the original mailing letter as a bonus or incentive for attending, when it could easily have been so – particularly if they had given it a value.

My estimate was that it could easily have been sold for around £100.

So Jim could have chosen to include it as a bonus for attendance – or even sold it at the back of the room. The event and presentation was easily high quality enough that some people attending would have purchased it there and then.

And this is a really important point. Whilst we are all encouraged to constantly be posting content onto social media platforms, blogs and our websites – some content should be saved for our events and for products that people will purchase.

In the case of Jim's Special Report, it added a great deal of extra value to his event but could also have produced additional revenue.

My personal view is that we are going a bit over the top on the incessant drive to post free content, and whilst this has its place, we are often missing opportunities to monetise our best work – which will have most appeal when made available at live events.

The Follow Up

Lunch exceeded expectations and after a cheery goodbye from Jim, I made my way home. There were no feedback forms to complete, but in fact I think their inclusion might have 'cheapened' the event slightly. It was clear from the audience reaction that it had gone well, and perhaps any feedback would be requested at a later date, on the phone or by email.

There was no further contact from Jones and Co that day, and after having found the seminar valuable and enjoyable, I would certainly have not objected to receiving a quick follow up message later in the afternoon – be it a text message or email.

All it needed to say was *"Philip – thank you so much for joining us today; it would be great to stay in touch. Kind regards Jim"*

A bonus point missed.

However, four days later I received a nice letter from Jones and Co thanking me again and inviting me to register for their email newsletter and other updates. I was more than happy to do so.

After that, there was no further direct contact from Jim and his team, which surprised me. I don't actually know how many attendees at their event went on to become clients, but as mentioned I estimate just over fifty percent on the day.

The seminar was good enough quality that I would certainly have been open to a telephone discussion about moving things forward and appointing them as my financial adviser.

Summary

The first point to make is that you don't have to hire a country house hotel. Spending a lot of money on your venue is not, on its own going to get you new clients/customers.

What is important is that you choose somewhere that is relevant to your audience and is a little bit different. Use your imagination on this or work with a venue finding service.

Your own office or premises can be just as good, particularly if it gives attendees the opportunity to see behind the scenes of what you do or how you make things.

Or look out for other local businesses who have interesting premises. I recently discovered a small local gin distillery who make their premises available for small events, with the presentation space being right in the middle of the manufacturing area.

But from the example I have given, the main point to note is how the smallest detail can add or take away from the success of your event – whether it's the way the mailing letter is presented, the welcome (or lack of it) on the door or the follow up afterwards, all these points and many others can make the difference between winning or losing a potential client.

The Future

As I write, live streaming on Facebook and LinkedIn is all the rage – giving seminar and event hosts a further amazing opportunity to spread their expertise far and wide.

Imagine hosting your seminar live at a local venue, but simultaneously streaming it to your friends and connections online, thus dramatically expanding your reach. The potential for this is immense, and very much to be recommended if you plan to use live marketing as part of your overall communication strategy.

Those businesses who will benefit most, will be those who are strategic in their approach to using this technology, but even those who experiment have potentially much to gain.

It will be important to try out different formats for streaming your event, because first and foremost your seminar or workshop has been designed for those who attend it live and in person. So to get the best out of live streaming, presenters will also want to think carefully about how they also engage with their online audience.

It is still fairy early days for live streaming of seminars by small businesses, but I suspect we will see rapid take up of this approach. What's more the live streaming technology is free to use – including tools such as Restream which currently allow you to stream to thirty or more different social media platforms.

And then we have Virtual and Augmented Reality…

Imagine attending a seminar where you don't have to travel anywhere, but where you can still be part of the event in full 3D!

Virtual reality gaming is commonplace, but to date it is not widely being used in the event space. But we are increasingly seeing large conferences and stage shows where a speaker or performer is 'projected' virtually onto the stage as a hologram, thus saving travel costs and significantly reducing the carbon footprint of the event.

The cost of such technology is currently well outside the budget of most small businesses, but it's something to look forward to for the future.

That said, recording your own seminar or workshop and then making it available through a virtual reality headset is most certainly within reach of more and more businesses.

Whatever the future holds for live business events and seminars, I for one, am incredibly excited about it.

Taking Action

What three things have you most got out of this book?

1.

2.

3.

How do you see the contents of this book specifically helping your business?

1.

2.

3.

What are your immediate goals for applying the content of this book?

1.

2.

3.

When are you going to get started…?!

1.

Message from the Author

I really appreciate you reading this book – thank you. I hope that you have found it fun, enjoyable and useful.

In turn, I've thoroughly enjoyed updating it from the original version first written in 2003, and I've been amazed at how technology has both changed and enhanced the seminar marketing process.

Please write to me to let me know how you get on planning, promoting and presenting your own seminars – I love to hear readers' stories and experiences. And why not send me a photo of your event – or tag me at @philipcalvert on Twitter.

If you have enjoyed this book, please help me to spread the message further by giving it a Five Star review on Amazon.

Thanks in advance…

Philip Calvert

Interested in purchasing ten or more copies of this book?

Contact us for information on special discounts available for bulk purchases: philip@philipcalvert.com

Interested in having Philip Calvert speak at your conference or event?

Philip speaks at conferences worldwide, so for an entertaining, high content presentation or keynote speech with actionable takeaways, book Philip today.

You should contact Philip using the email address above or visit his website at www.philipcalvert.com or LinkedIn profile at www.linkedin.com/in/saleskeynotespeaker

About the Author

Philip Calvert - Delivering Actionable Ideas to Make a Positive Impact at your Conference, Corporate Event or Sales Meeting.

Philip is an international speaker and author specialising in helping financial advice businesses to market and present themselves with credibility and professionalism through seminars, live events, public speaking, LinkedIn and wider social media.

A world leading authority on LinkedIn and Seminar Selling, Philip speaks worldwide and delivers high value and entertaining keynotes and breakout sessions.

For further information connect with him on LinkedIn at www.linkedin.com/in/saleskeynotespeaker or send an email to philip@philipcalvert.com.

Visit his website at www.philipcalvert.com

Disclaimer and Terms of Use

This book is provided for research and educational purposes. You do not have resell rights or giveaway rights to any portion of this publication. Only customers that have purchased this publication are authorised to view it. No part of this publication may be transmitted or reproduced in any way without the prior written permission of the author. Violations of this copyright will be enforced in law.

The information services and resources provided in this book are based upon the current internet marketing and economic environment. The techniques presented have been extraordinarily lucrative and rewarding to information marketers and business owners worldwide, however because the internet is constantly changing, some sites and services presented in this book may change, cease or expand with time.

We hope that the skills and knowledge acquired from this book will provide you with the ability to adapt to inevitable internet and marketing evolution. However, we cannot be held responsible for changes that may affect the applicability or effectiveness of these techniques.

Any earnings, income statements or other results quoted, are based on our own and the testing of other marketers and are estimates of what we believe you could earn. There is no assurance you will do as well as stated in any examples and could be influenced by a variety of factors, not least of which include work ethic and market conditions. If you rely upon any figures provided, you must accept the entire risk of not doing as well as the information provided.

All product names, logos and artwork mentioned in this book are copyrights of their respective owners. None of the owners have sponsored or endorsed this publication.

While all attempts have been made to verify information provided, the author assumes no responsibility for errors, omissions or contrary interpretation on the subject matter herein. Any perceived slights of people or organisations are unintentional. The purchaser or reader of this publication assumes responsibility for the use of these materials and information.

No guarantees of income are made. The author reserves the right to make changes and assumes no responsibility or liability whatsoever on behalf of any purchaser or reader of these materials.

From time to time, the author has included hyperlinks to external products and services, some of which may be an affiliate link, where the author would receive a commission should the reader make a purchase.

The purchaser and reader assume full responsibility for compliance and compliant use of the material in this book, as defined by their respective regulatory body. No guarantees are made by the author that any of the ideas presented in this book will be acceptable under the purchaser or reader's local compliance regime.

Notes

Copyright Philip Calvert 2019. All Rights Reserved.

Printed in Great
Britain
by Amazon